Religion and the Search
for New Ideals
in the USSR

Religion and the Search for New Ideals in the USSR

Edited by

WILLIAM C. FLETCHER

and

ANTHONY J. STROVER

Published for the
Institute for the Study of the USSR

FREDERICK A. PRAEGER, *Publishers*
New York • Washington • London

FREDERICK A. PRAEGER, *Publishers*
111 Fourth Avenue, New York, N.Y. 10003, U.S.A.
77-79 Charlotte Street, London W.1, England

Published in the United States of America in 1967
by Frederick A. Praeger, Inc., Publishers

Library of Congress Catalog Card Number: 67-16683

This book is Number 187 in the series
Praeger Publications in Russian History and World Communism

Printed in the United States of America

PAUL B. ANDERSON, a graduate of the University of Iowa, was in Russia during the Bolshevik Revolution of 1917, and directed the Russian YMCA press in Paris in 1921. He is consultant to the Center for Research and Study of Religious Institutions in Geneva, to the World Alliance, YMCA, Geneva, and to the National Council of Churches, New York. He is the author of *Russia's Religious Future* (1935) and *People, State and Church in Modern Russia* (1944).

WILLIAM C. FLETCHER, a graduate of the University of California, Los Angeles, received a B.D. degree from the California Baptist Theological Seminary and a Ph.D. degree in church history from the University of Southern California. Now director of the Center for Research and Study of Religious Institutions in Geneva, he is the author of *A Study in Survival: The Church in Russia, 1927–1943* (1965) and of a forthcoming volume, *Nikolai: Biography of an Enigma* and the compiler of *Christianity in the Soviet Union: An Annotated Bibliography* (1963).

MAX HAYWARD, a fellow of St. Antony's College, Oxford, is the co-translator of Boris Pasternak's *Doctor Zhivago* (1958) and of Alexander Solzhenitsyn's *One Day in the Life of Ivan Denisovich* (1963) and *For the Good of the Cause* (1964), and co-editor of *Soviet Literature in the Sixties* (1964). He translated and edited *On Trial: The Soviet State versus "Abram Tertz" and "Nikolai Arzhak"* (1966).

The Rev. DMITRY KONSTANTINOV was a printer and publisher in the Soviet Union before World War II. Now a priest of the Russian Orthodox Church in the United States, he contributes articles on religious subjects to publications of the Institute for the Study of the USSR.

HANS LAMM, a native of Munich, received an M.S.W. degree from Washington University, St. Louis, Missouri, and a Ph.D. degree in philosophy from the University of Erlangen. Since 1940, he has been engaged in journalism and has been active in Jewish organizational work. He is a departmental head at the Münchner Volkshochschule.

PETER B. REDDAWAY, a graduate of Cambridge University, has engaged in advanced studies at Harvard, Moscow, and London universities and is a lecturer in government at the London School of Economics. His articles have appeared in *Survey* and in *Soviet Studies* (Glasgow). He is co-editor (with Leonard B. Schapiro) of a forthcoming volume, *Lenin After Fifty Years*.

HEINRICH SCHULZ was graduated from a Russian medical institute in 1931 and practiced as a physician and worked in various Soviet research centers before leaving the Soviet Union in 1943. A staff member of the Institute for the Study of the USSR since 1951, he became its director in 1959. He is the author of many publications dealing with Soviet medicine and health services and is an associate of the Russian Institute of Fordham University.

ZINAIDA SHAKHOVSKAYA studied at the American College in Istanbul and at the Collège de France in Paris. She received French and Belgian decorations for her work as a war correspondent and was awarded the Prix de Paris (1949) and the Prix Therouanne of the Académie Française (1964) for her numerous books. Since 1960, she has been on the staff of Radiotélévision Française.

GEORG A. VON STACKELBERG, a specialist on Central and South Asian affairs, is a regular contributor to the publications of the Institute for the Study of the USSR.

ANTHONY STROVER, a gradute of Cambridge University in Russian language and Soviet area studies, is coordinating editor, in charge of the English-language publications section, of the Institute for the Study of the USSR.

NIKITA STRUVE, an associate lecturer at the Sorbonne, Paris, is a specialist on Soviet religious affairs.

NADEZHDA TEODOROVICH, a doctor of psychiatry, worked in various Soviet welfare institutions and was active in church work during the 1930's. A specialist on East European religious affairs, she is a member of the research staff of the Institute for the Study of the USSR.

GUSTAV WETTER, S.J., was for many years the Superior of the Collegium Russicum in Rome, the famed Jesuit institution devoted to the study of East European problems, and is now professor of the history of Russian philosophy at the Vatican Institute of Oriental Studies in Rome. His *Dialectical Materialism* (1958) is widely regarded as the standard work on the subject. His most recent work in English is *Soviet Ideology Today* (1966).

Contents

Editorial Note

From Soviet books, journals, and other publications, it is apparent that important elements in Soviet society are dissatisfied with the officially promulgated tenets of Marxism-Leninism and are searching for an alternative to what they consider an obsolescing ideology. In order to assess the role that religion is playing in this process, the Institute for the Study of the USSR in Munich, Germany, held an international symposium from April 25 to 27, 1966. Specialists from seven countries, including representatives of the Christian Churches, Islam, and Judaism, took part. The chapters of this volume grew out of the papers presented to the symposium and their discussion.

Communism and the Problem of Intellectual Freedom

Gustav Wetter

Shortly after the end of the war, in the spring of 1946, I had the opportunity of talking with a group of Italian communist intellectuals. One of them, Prof. Geymonat, asked me why the Catholic Church exhibits such determined opposition to communism. I was astonished at his question, and replied that this was fairly obvious, since communism subscribed to materialism and atheism. But Prof. Geymonat described this view as a gross misconception: Marxism was merely a positive science, like medicine, biology or mathematics, but dealing with the transformation of society; it had nothing to do with philosophy, world outlook or religion. Just as a man could be a good doctor and hold any one of a variety of philosophies of life, so it was possible to be a Marxist and subscribe to any philosophy, any religion, or to none at all. I was very astonished at this opinion of an Italian communist, as from the Soviet standpoint of those days—and even of today—such an attitude was an outright heresy. In the Soviet view this would mean restricting Marxism to the realm of historical materialism and removing it from its philosophical foundation of dialectical materialism. But this is completely unacceptable, since the two are inseparably linked together.

This applies to the Soviet standpoint up to the present time. But must it always be so, and will it always be so? Would it not be conceivable that even the Soviets may some day get to the point where only economic and social life is based on a Marxist foundation, and the unhappy intermingling of Marxism with philosophy of life is abandoned? Have there not been certain processes discernible in the Soviet Union of late, that point in this direction? I refer here in particular to the trend towards greater objectivity that has been characteristic of the Soviet leadership since the fall of Khrushchev, to events such as the removal of Ilyichev from office as head of the ideological section of the Central Committee, to the fact that Soviet ideology has ventured in recent years into a number of new sciences, such as empirical sociology, social psychology, information theory, cybernetics, etc.

Then there are certain processes within world communism which may exercise an influence in the same direction on developments in the Soviet Union. In Yugoslavia the Communist League has amended its statutes so that membership in the Party and membership of a religion are no longer mutually exclusive. About a year ago legal protection for religion was reinforced; now anybody who deprives another of his rights because of his religious views is guilty of a punishable offence. At its last Party Congress in January this year, the Italian Communist Party advanced the dialogue with the Catholics to the Party line and dissociated itself, in the interests of this dialogue, from any "automatic atheism." It now disapproves of any State which "grants any ideology, philo-

1

sophy or religion or any cultural or artistic school special privileges to the detriment of others." A few weeks ago the French Communist Party followed the example of its Italian brothers and declared itself officially in favour of freedom in art and religion. Is it not conceivable that such changes within these communist parties might, despite the Soviet Communist Party's claim to supreme leadership, also affect the attitude of the Soviet leaders and, together with the internal Soviet trends already mentioned, help to bring about a new attitude towards philosophy of life inside the Soviet Union, an attitude comparable to that of Prof. Geymonat in Turin?

The object of this opening paper is therefore to examine firstly how the question of the relationship between Marxism and philosophy of life presents itself from the communist viewpoint and whether there are any aspects of Soviet Marxist ideology that might develop towards a dissociation of Marxist economic and social theory on the one hand from the general philosophy of life on the other, and secondly what difficulties this ideology puts in the way of such dissociation.

In this examination we shall be concerned primarily—in line with the overall theme of our symposium—with Soviet communism. However, we cannot altogether ignore the attitude of non-Soviet communist parties, because we cannot exclude *a priori* all possibility of their affecting the Soviet Communist Party and because their outlook may perhaps be viewed in certain Soviet quarters as an alternative attitude.

A first question that needs clarifying is what we understand by "communism." In our context "communism" does not mean a form of society, such as when "communism" is designated as the second and last phase in the establishment of a classless society and as used in reference to the transition from socialism to communism. Nor does communism here mean any mere doctrine. When we talk of "communism" in this present context, we use the term to cover all social and political movements which, in one form or another, subscribe to Marxism-Leninism. This immediately draws a clear distinction between communism in our sense and "Marxism," in that communism represents a special form of Marxism, namely the type of Marxism as extended and defined by Lenin.

When we accept the word "communism" in this sense, we see at once that it covers a great multitude of often widely divergent movements. These can be divided into two rough groups: firstly communism in those countries in which the communist party is in sole possession of the political power, that is, the Soviet Union, the countries of the People's Democracies including Yugoslavia, China and Cuba; and secondly, communism in the free world.

Between these two main varieties of communism there are often considerable differences, even though all recognize in one way or another the doctrines not only of Marx but also of Lenin. To investigate wherein the individual differences between the two main streams lie is beyond our present scope. As a general guide, however, it may be said that, through having to deal with an opponent who is not restricted in the free expression of his views, the communist move-

2

ments in the free world have been forced to interpret the doctrines of the classical exponents in a much more flexible manner, so as to prevent it from becoming too apparent how scientifically untenable many of these doctrines are. To quote only one concrete point of particular significance in regard to the question of the relationship between Marxism and philosophy of life: among communist philosophers in the free world, particularly in countries like Italy and France, there will certainly not be many who would seriously subscribe to Engels' doctrine of dialectics in nature. But if dialectics in nature is rejected, the whole system of dialectical materialism of the Soviet variety collapses. For such philosophers Marxist philosophy then often means nothing more than a Marxist humanism on an economic foundation or a historicism as in Italy, if indeed they do not turn to some non-Marxist philosophy, such as logical positivism.

But even within the two main camps of communism mentioned above, closer inspection reveals considerable differences. This applies not only to the communist movements in the free world, but also to those countries where the communist party holds power. Here dialectical and historical materialism constitute the ruling ideology as officially propagated. However, this does not rule out the possibility that in certain countries, such as above all Poland and Yugoslavia, but also to a certain extent in countries like Hungary and Czechoslovakia, many theorists—including those who definitely subscribe to Marxism-Leninism—behave in very arbitrary fashion with this doctrine and often depart from it on many important points, even sometimes coming very close to a rejection of dialectical materialism of the Engels variety. In addition, there are often considerable differences in political practice. Here we need only think of the Moscow-Peking conflict, the background to which is almost exclusively a matter of practical politics and only to a small extent of ideology. The often very considerable differences in the matter of policies towards religion, which are of such particular importance in our context, have already been mentioned briefly.

Despite all these nuances, these movements still have so much in common that they can be grouped together under the heading "communism."

Secondly we must ask whether the doctrine on which communism bases its action and to which every adherent of this movement must subscribe—and recognition of which is demanded in communist-ruled countries not only from Party members but also from the entire population—whether this doctrine does in fact constitute a valid philosophy of life or merely a collection of economic, social and political theories.

Before attempting to answer this question, we must clarify the expression "philosophy of life." The term means more than a synoptic view of the world based on the discoveries of the individual sciences, particularly the natural sciences, a view which ignores the ultimate, metaphysical questions relating to the essence and meaning of the world. "Philosophy of life," however, means this very overall view of essence and value, meaning and purpose of the world in general and of human life in particular.

3

When we apply these definitions to today's Marxism-Leninism, it immediately becomes clear that it does not contain merely a collection of economic and social theories, but also constitutes both an independent view of the world and a genuine philosophy of life. The creation of this view of the world encompassing society and nature was above all the work of Engels. Marx dealt more with social and economic questions. In elaborating the materialistic interpretation of history which forms the nucleus of historical materialism he was concerned with discovering the factor which ultimately determines the entire social development of mankind in history. He thought he had found it in the way in which men produce the necessities of life. According to Marx, the evolution of the manner of production reveals a periodically recurring contradiction between the level of development of a society's forces of production and the outdated social conditions of production, a contradiction which finds its resolution in a revolutionary transformation of the form of society. To throw light on how this contradiction functioned in capitalistic society was the lode-star which guided Marx in all his economic studies leading to the writing of *Capital*. The natural sciences interested him less.

Somewhere about the seventies of the last century, Engels set out to apply the dialectical law of evolution which Marx had propounded for the social realm to the world of nature and to show that the evolution of nature is also actuated by the formation and resolution of contradictions leading to the creation of a succession of new forms and species. Thus, in elaborating his "dialectics of nature" it was his chief aim to show that the entire range of individual facts unites to form one great whole, a complex not of self-contained things defined for all time, but a complex of processes in which everything remains so to speak in a state of flux, with one thing emerging from another and in turn developing into something else.

Even for Engels and therefore also in the present-day Soviet ideology, this synopsis had the function not only of a view of the world but also of a genuine philosophy of life. The attempt at a materialistic interpretation of the world was designed to convince the consciousness of men that they should not look to any supernatural higher being for liberation and salvation, but should fight for these themselves. Here the proof that the dialectical law of contradiction and conflict between opposites did not apply only to the social realm, but also to nature and hence to all reality, was to give mankind the comforting assurance that there are no eternal and unalterable things in this world, that the existing social order would also come to an end some time; also, this law was intended to make the oppressed aware of the necessity for revolutionary conflict: if evolution is furthered everywhere in the world, and even in nature, by conflict between opposites, the same must apply to social evolution; only through conflict could society win through to a brighter future.

In this way the Marxist doctrine became a view of the world and a philosophy of life that was so much of a piece that it exercised a fascination over many, particularly over the scientifically untrained and the semi-educated. Marxism claims to have a doctrine which can provide an answer to all questions and which helps mankind to cope with any situation. And in addition to offering man a guide to the surrounding world, this doctrine claims to give him information on the meaning and purpose of life, this meaning being so to live and to fight that all alienation of man and all injustice is removed and a social order established in which all men can develop their own personality to the utmost.

That Marxism of the Engels variety has not lost its philosophical character in Leninism is shown in Lenin's polemics against deviationist movements within Russian Marxism, in particular in his fight against empiriocriticism. As the ultimate criterion for the assessment and condemnation of deviationist views Lenin often uses the argument that this doctrine would lead to "fideism" and "clericalism." However, according to Lenin and Leninism, the reason why these philosophies of life should be combatted is not that Marxism should be set up against them as a science without a philosophy of life, but that Marxism has its own "scientific" philosophy of life opposed to religion.

We have already mentioned that a process of departure from Engels' dialectics in nature is discernible among communist theorists in certain countries. Sometimes this departure from the system of dialectical and even historical materialism goes so far that Marxism is stated to be merely a method of scientific exploration of the phenomena of social life. Often the departure from Engels' dialectics of nature is coupled with a return to the philosophical thinking of the younger Marx. For such theorists Marxism then comes to mean primarily a humanism on an economic basis. Since Marx's early thinking is today acquiring increasing importance even within the communist realm, the essential outline of the young Marx's humanism should obviously be sketched here.

Like many of his contemporaries, Marx was disturbed by the realization that man in the modern world is increasingly becoming the slave of his own labours. In all his fields of activity, in the economic, social, political and ideological field, the creations of man turn into powers which escape further and further from the control of their creator, enslave him and threaten his existence. How can this dehumanized world, in which things are the rulers, be turned back into a world of human beings, in which man rules and where mutual relations are not those between things but between human beings? Feuerbach had attributed this "alienation" of man from himself to the phenomenon of religion. In religion, particularly in the Christian religion, man sets up against his own being another being whom he idealizes, to which he ascribes everything which he would like to be but does not find within himself. He calls this being God and submits himself to it. The more he ascribes to this being, the less he retains for himself. Thus to arrive at the real man who is master of himself, this alienation of man must be removed.

But Marx goes further than Feuerbach. He asks how this alienation of man in religion arose, and he considers he has found the answer in a similar alienation of man in the economic and social field. Man creates a false consciousness of the world in his religion because he constitutes such a false world in his own (material) existence. But what is responsible for this alienation of man in the economic and social field? What in fact does "alienation" of man mean? One can only speak of alienation when one has a definition for man's being. In what does Marx see this being of man?

In defining the being of man Marx once again reveals himself to be entirely the child of his times. Whereas in idealism the being of man was seen in one way or another in free self-determination, Marx turns this idea into the materialistic and sees the being of man in a dialectical process of self-creation taking place in the production of the material necessities of life, that is, in work. For Marx, to produce means to draw something out of oneself. Thus, in his work man turns his own being into objective reality in the shape of his product. This objectification, however, is followed by a fresh subjectification when man uses the product to sustain his own material life. Work is thus seen as a process of self-creation by man, a *dialectical* process in that this self-creation—i.e., self-materialization—takes place via a self-expenditure and objectification seen in the transfer of the being of man into his product.

In the present form of society based on the division of labour and private property, however, the product created by man, and hence his own objectified being, becomes somebody else's private property. It thus not only remains fixed in the state of objectification, but also becomes—in the form of capital—a power that is hostile to the actual producer and hence oppresses him. The more of himself a worker gives out, the more goods and values he creates, the more impoverished he himself becomes, and the more powerful becomes the hostile world of capital opposing him. Thus, Marx sees the "alienation of man from the product of his labours" as the most fundamental of all forms of man's alienation. As the next stage comes the alienation of man from his work itself. This finds expression in the fact that in the present order man regards work, which as a process of self-creation, ought to be a necessity of life to him, as an oppressive burden; this is why he feels unhappy at work, and happy and himself only when away from work. This "alienation of the worker from his work" then develops further into a "self-alienation," since for Marx, as we have seen, work constitutes the real being of man. However, when Marx talks here of "man," it should be remembered that he is always thinking of what he calls the "social man," so that for him the being of man means a "generic being." In this way self-alienation necessarily becomes alienation between men, alienation of man from man, which finds expression in the fact that, in an order based on private property, relations between men are dehumanized; they cease to be personal relationships and become relationships between things. And finally all these forms of the alienation of man have their repercussions in the political realm, where the social man sets up against his own social being an outside being in the form of the State, as well as in the spiritual realm where, as we have already seen, man sets up against his own being the notion of a God, an outside being governing him.

Thus in order to arrive at the true man it is not sufficient, as Feuerbach claimed, to remove religious alienation. The axe must be laid at the root of all alienation, which Marx saw in private property. This takes place through the revolution of the proletariat and through the establishment of communism. Hence for Marx, communism means not only the removal of the exploitation of man by man, but also the overcoming of all forms of the alienation of man. It means not only overcoming the conflict between man and man, but also overcoming the conflict between man and nature! Only through the removal of all alienation of man can the humanization of nature occurring in the action of production come into full effect. For Marx, then, communism is "perfect naturalism = humanism, perfect humanism = naturalism; it is the true solution of the conflict between man and nature, and between man and man, the true solution of the conflict between existence and being, between freedom and necessity, between individual and genus. It is the solution to the riddle of history and knows itself to be this solution."

These words of Marx show clearly that communism for him meant much more than a particular form of economy and a special system of society. In these views, which he wrote down in 1844, the term communism covered a complete view of the world as well as a special conception of the meaning and purpose of human existence. Hence these views, too, must be classified as a philosophy of life.

But was this also the view of the older and more mature Marx, of the author of *Capital*, who originated the school of Marxism? The "Economico-Philosophical Manuscripts from the Year 1844," the main source for his alienation doctrine, and from which the synopsis of communism quoted above is taken, remained unpublished until 1932. This might suggest that Marx did not consider them worthy of publication, that he in a sense disowned them.

The question of the relationship between the young and the mature Marx and of which is the "true" Marx, the young Marx of the early writings and the speculations on alienation, or the mature Marx of *Capital*, is a highly controversial problem. In the Soviet Union the mature Marx is usually regarded as the "true" Marx. However, one interesting interpretation is that of Adam Schaff, a member of the Central Committee of the Polish Communist Party and leading philosopher of Polish communism. Schaff rejects all attemts to construct a contrast between the young and the mature Marx and holds the view that the works of the later Marx are to be interpreted in the light of the humanism of the early Marx.

We cannot, of course, enter into a discussion of these views here. However, as regards our question of whether Marxism is to be regarded as a philosophy of life, we can draw the following conclusion: to the extent to which present Marxism takes its direction from the humanism of the young Marx, it becomes a real philosophy of life. The opposite holds good only when Engels' dialectical materialism and early Marxist humanism are discarded, and Marxism is interpreted either as a purely economic and social concept without a philosophical foundation of its own, or when, as is also to be observed in certain quarters, an attempt is made to give it a philosophical basis in logical positivism.

7

A special question in this connection is whether the Marxist philosophy of life, either of Marxist-Leninist brand or in the form inspired by the thinking of the young Marx, is essentially atheistic. This question is of particular interest in regard to religion. It might almost appear to be an unnecessary question, since to many people the atheistic content of the Marxist philosophy of life seems to be self-evident. Yet the view has been expressed that atheism is not an essential component of Marxist doctrine, but merely a trimming added by contemporary circumstances. It was argued that the atheistic note in the Marxist doctrine was due merely to the political situation at the time when Marx began his activities, when, because of the alliance between the Church of those days and absolutism, the political struggle of the working class against absolutism necessarily had to expand into a struggle against the Church as well.

The question takes a different turn for Marxist-Leninism of the Soviet brand, in which dialectical materialism in the form created primarily by Engels and further elaborated by Lenin has become a mandatory component of ideology, and for those movements within today's communism which are detaching themselves from Engels' dialectics of nature and turning back to the thinking of the young Marx for inspiration.

The essentially atheistic nature of dialectical (and historical) materialism of the present-day Soviet variety appears to be fairly obvious. Historical materialism declares religion to be that form of superstructure that is furthest removed from the real basis of social events and thus presents reality essentially in distorted form. Therefore, as soon as social existence is healthy, and all exploitation of man by man, together with all alienation of man, has been removed, there will be no more religion.

Following the relativization of religion in historical materialism, the attempt is made in dialectical materialism to fill the vacuum thus created with new, atheistic content. To avoid having to assume the creation of the world, dialectical materialism sets up the thesis of the eternity of the material world and quotes natural science to substantiate this thesis; the eternity of the world is alleged to have been proved by science. However, if we ask the scientists themselves about this point, we get the answer that at the present stage of development the question cannot be decided. Yet dialectical materialism presents this view not as a hypothesis, but as an accepted thesis. It does not hold to it, however, because of any process of reasoning, but because of an arbitrary decision based on atheistic emotions. Thus, whereas historical materialism sets out to show that man has no need of God as a redeemer, dialectical materialism also tries to prove that nature does not need him as a creator.

The abandonment of Engels' dialectics of nature and hence of modern dialectical materialism through a return to the young Marx in no way changes the essentially atheistic nature of the Marxist philosophy of life. The point of departure for the young Marx's doctrine of alienation was, after all, Feuerbach's criticism of religion, whose results Marx appropriated and sought to expand. The idea of "self-creation by man" thus also radically excludes the idea of God. And finally, the whole doctrine of the different forms of alienation has no other purpose but to show how man can be rooted solely in himself. This means, however, that he is enclosed in immanence, and any opening towards transcendence is cut off at the root.

As a result of our examination so far we can say that communism does in essence constitute an independent philosophy of life and that, at any rate in so far as communism regards historical *and* dialectical materialism as a mandatory basis for its ideology or—in the various degrees of rejection of dialectical materialism—in so far as it grounds itself on the humanism of the young Marx, this philosophy of life is atheistic.

This raises a further question, however, and a decisive one: does this necessarily lead to conflict with other philosophies of life on the level of practical life, or is it conceivable that communism might come to accept a situation in which only its own Party members subscribed to this philosophy and the rest of the people living within its realm held different views? Might it be conceivable that communists and those of other outlooks might in time live side by side in a communist-ruled country, just as members of different religions and confessions live side by side in *one* State? After all, there were times when the latter warred against each other to the knife. Yet today they have come to tolerate one another.

At first glance it might seem that such peaceful coexistence of different philosophies of life even within a communist-ruled country should certainly be possible on the basis of Marxist-Leninist ideology. The materialistic conception of history teaches that religion—and the same applies to other non-Marxist philosophies of life—is an illusory consciousness of the world, which is the expression of an unhealthy socio-economic existence. Therefore it will necessarily die out as soon as social existence becomes healthy and generates a correct social conciousness. In this connection Lenin, too, declared that the principal weapon in the battle against religion must be the creation of a healthy form of society, which will cut off the social roots from which religion springs and thus cause it to die. Then there is another Marxist-Leninist principle which would appear to offer the possibility of peaceful coexistence between different philosophies of life within a communist-ruled country. This is the proposition that religion is a private affair. Lenin interpreted this proposition as being valid only from the point of view of the State, not from that of the Communist Party, which was required to combat religion as an unscientific philosophy of life. This, however, is tantamount to admitting that the State should maintain a neutral attitude towards religion—and by the same token towards any other philosophy of life—that the Party should not use State resources in its fight against religion.

Consequently, as we have already seen, responsible representatives of communist parties in the free world have of late spoken out firmly against the use of force against religion. For example, when the Central Committee of the Communist Party of the Soviet Union decided at the end of 1963 at the instigation of Leonid Ilyichev to step up the fight against religion, Roger Garaudy, member of the Politburo of the French Communist Party and the most important philo-

9

sopher in French communism, branded Ilyichev's methods as "idealistic," as they aimed at bringing about the death of religion by acting on the consciousness of man rather than by changing social existence as required by historical materialism. Similar voices are also to be heard among Yugoslav communists. And we have already mentioned the resolutions of the Italian Party Congress in favour of an ideologically neutral State.

Nevertheless the fact remains that in all communist-ruled countries, not excluding Yugoslavia, non-Marxist philosophies have been repressed by force and by the use of State powers right down to the recent past. Even the prohibition of religious publicity, not only in the Soviet Union, but also even in Yugoslavia, is a form of obstruction to other philosophies of life applied through State powers. The question therefore arises of whether this fact is to be qualified merely as an inconsistency in practice, a deviation from basic principles, or whether it has a more fundamental significance. Are there conditions inherent in the basic principles which of necessity give rise to a situation of conflict between Marxist and other philosophies in communist-ruled countries?

Such conditions do in fact exist. One of the first of them is the principle of unity between theory and practice which holds good for all forms of Marxism. As we have seen, communism regards its theory not only as a purely economic, social or political theory, but as an all-inclusive philosophy of life, including the question of the meaning and purpose of the whole of human existence. Thus if it is to remain true to itself, it cannot refrain from fashioning the conditions of life—not only the whole social and economic scene, but also cultural life as well—along its own lines wherever this is possible. The Soviet Communist Party regards its own history as "Marxism-Leninism in action" or as the "incarnation" of Marxism-Leninism. It therefore cannot admit that any aspect of life in the society it directs should permanently remain outside this "incarnation." It may at times refrain for tactical reasons from pushing this "incarnation" too far, particularly if the use of force would produce exactly the opposite effect. This explains why religion is tolerated in the Soviet Union and other communist-ruled countries. It also explains a characteristic feature of this toleration, namely the effort to confine religion and the Church to the holding of religious services and to forbid all social and cultural activity and all publicity. This attitude also entails a great temptation to intervene, should—contrary to all Marxist forecasts—religion in socialist countries fail to show signs of dying out, and to bring about by force what history does not accomplish by itself.

Then there is a second and perhaps even more decisive reason. The power of the communist party in communist-ruled countries as the only party and the major force in social life is based, in essence, on Marxist-Leninist ideology. Thus, if the Party were to tolerate the existence of other philosophies of life within its realm, it would *ipso facto* open the door for a possible challenge to its power and privilege.

The dominating and all-embracing role of the Party is based primarily on the typical Leninist extension of the Marxist doctrine or, to be more precise, of historical materialism. Marx and Engels regarded the working *class* as the decisive force which would bring about socialism. Even when they talked of an organization or party, they envisaged an organization of the entire working class. The formation of an elite, rigid discipline and the authority of a ruling class were categorically rejected. It was Lenin who shifted the emphasis from class to Party as the former's vanguard. In his eyes, the role of the Party was two-fold: firstly its task is to give the working class a genuinely socialist consciousness. Left to themselves the workers, according to Lenin, would get no further than the formation of a trade unionistic consciousness. As modern socialism, however, is a science, the workers can only be given this consciousness "from outside." The Party's second task is to march at the head of the class in the revolutionary battle. But this is only possible if it is subjected to rigid discipline. In harmony with this the communist party in the Soviet Union sees itself as "a voluntary association of like-minded men and women who have banded together to put the Marxist philosophy into practice and to fulfil the historic mission of the working class."[1] All this, however, does not apply only to the period before the conquest of power. "Experience in socialist countries has shown that the importance of the Marxist party as the leader of the working class and of all other workers not only does not diminish after the revolution, but even grows immeasurably. The Marxist Party now bears responsibility for everything that takes place in society, for the policies of the State as a dictatorship of the proletariat, for the development of the forces of production and of culture and for the growth of general prosperity."[2]

This view of the role of the communist party thus rests on a typical Lenin concept, different from those of Marx and Engels. Nevertheless, it is inconceivable without the Marx-Engels concept of historical materialism as the foundation of the "historic mission" of the working class, a mission which consists not only in overthrowing the present ruling class but also in destroying all future division of the classes at the root through the abolition of private property. But this again is no longer Lenin's contribution, but traditional Marxist doctrine.

Nevertheless, it might be asked here whether historical materialism, i.e., the socio-scientific portion of Marxist ideology, does not already provide sufficient ideological justification for the Party's privileged position, and whether in fact dialectical materialism as a general philosophy of life is needed as well. What, for example, has the thesis of dialectical materialism concerning the infinity of the universe in space to do with the privileged position of the Party?

Obviously not every thesis of dialectical materialism is of direct import for the Party doctrine. Yet dialectical materialism is of great significance in safeguarding the Party's rulership. Soviet ideology holds the view that there is an inner unity between dialectical and historical materialism, in that historical materialism is merely the application of the basic principles of dialectical materialism to the realm of social evolution in history. Needless to say, it is possible to dis-

---

[1] *Grundlagen des Marxismus-Leninismus* (Fundamentals of Marxism-Leninism), Berlin, 1960, p. 389.
[2] *Ibid.*, p. 609.

agree on this point. In fact, examination is more likely to reveal that no such inevitable internal link exists. At the very least it could be contended that historical materialism can also stand on its own feet and is even tenable if dialectical materialism, in the form in which it was propounded by Engels, is rejected. The abandonment of dialectical materialism, however, would create a philosophical no-man's-land which would be extremely dangerous for the Party, since it could be occupied by all kinds of philosophical streams. And then the Party would always have to be prepared for persons within its realm to challenge its authority with the argument "it is more important to obey God than man." It is not for nothing, therefore, that the Soviet Communist Party identifies itself as an association of like-minded men and women "who have banded together to put the Marxist philosophy of life into effect."

Hence, although during the transition from the class society to socialism the existence side by side of different philosophies of life can be justified on the basis of Marx's doctrine of foundation and superstructure, the Party nevertheless has a vital interest in encouraging the gradual disappearance of other forms of social consciousness by using more or less gentle pressure. It is therefore not surprising that the Soviet leadership confines its indefatigable propaganda in favour of peaceful coexistence to the political and economic realm, while specifically excluding from it the realm of ideology. There can be no peaceful coexistence in the realm of ideology, as peaceful coexistence between truth and error is impossible; here only the call for inexorable warfare against bourgeois ideology is acceptable.

In conclusion, let us examine how far all that has been said goes towards answering our opening question, namely what prospects there are that the scattered changes to be observed in the attitude of various communist parties towards religion may develop towards an acceptance of the principle of a plurality of philosophies of life. In answer to this question I should like to cite the following points:

1. Those communist parties and movements which, like the Soviet Communist Party, regard dialectical materialism in the form propounded by Engels as a mandatory component of their ideology, necessarily bestow upon it the nature of a philosophy of life.

2. Even where dialectical materialism is discarded in favour of the humanism of the young Marx, these communist streams also continue to be essentially philosophies of like.

3. Communism would not cease to be an independent philosophy of life unless it saw its ideology as an economic and social science without philosophical implications, on the model of the other separate sciences.

4. As long as communism is in the nature of a philosophy of life, peaceful coexistence with other philosophies within the communist-ruled countries, though theoretically possible under Marxist-Leninist ideology, is very difficult to achieve in practice because of the claims of the communist party to absolute power.

12

The Problem of Alienation:
Life without Spiritual or Religious Ideals

Paul B. Anderson

Soviet philosophical literature of the last decade has paid a great deal of attention to the interest shown by the West in the Young Marx. *Problems of Philosophy* contains the full and finally edited text of one of the earliest Marxist classics, *Die Deutsche Ideologie (German Ideology)*.[1] The same journal also publishes a long explanatory article on the discovery of lost sections of the manuscript, the marginal notes by Marx and Engels, the successive drafts and the relation of *German Ideology* to preceding and subsequent works by Marx and Engels.[2] Importance is also attached to the month in which it was begun: November, not September, 1845.

Publication of this Marxist classic in 1965 was probably the result of completion of the editorial work and not of timing to fit topical interest; yet it is significant that *German Ideology*, which presents the earliest rounded statement of Marxist economic-materialistic philosophy, should be produced at the very height of a period of thoughtful analysis and criticism of one of its major points— alienation. For the same reason it provides a suitable introduction to this paper, in which we shall endeavour to give some sampling of Soviet interpretation of the relationship between Soviet and Western views on the subject.

Much of *German Ideology* could be quoted with profit to the understanding of Marx, but here we limit ourselves to a fairly lengthy excerpt from Section (18) on alienation. Marx and Engels evidently felt that Hegel had stopped inconclusively and part-way by not breaking with religion, and that Feuerbach, who violently rejected Christianity, did so on inadequate grounds: he posited hypothetical "man" and not "empirical, actively working" human beings:

> The social force, i.e., the compounded productive force, which appears as a result of the conditioned distribution of the labour and communal activity of a number of individuals, seems to the given individuals to be not their combined force—because their common activity comes about not voluntarily but instinctively—but something alien, outside them, regarding whose source and development they know nothing. Consequently they cannot master this force. On the contrary, the latter now passes through a series of its own phases and degrees of development, not only independent of the will and conduct of persons but, on the contrary, directing that will and conduct....

This *alienation* (italics and quotation marks are in the original text. P. B. A.) speaking in language used by philosophers, can be destroyed, of course, only by the

[1] *Voprosy filosofii*, No. 10, 1965, pp. 79–118; No. 11, 1965, pp. 111–37.
[2] G. A. Bagaturiya, "The Structure and Content of the Manuscript of the First Chapter of *Nemetskaya Ideologiya*, by K. Marx and F. Engels," *Voprosy filosofii*, No. 10, 1965, pp. 108–18.

presence of two *practical* presuppositions. In order to become an "unbearable" force, i.e., a force against which to revolt, it is essential that this alienation transform the basic mass of mankind into people completely "deprived of property," facing at the same time the existing world of wealth and education; both of these conditions assume a vast growth of productive force and a high degree of its development.... This development is a further essential presupposition because only along with this unusual development of productive force can a universal community of people be established....

Communism for us is not a *condition* which must be established, not an *ideal* according to which reality must be reconstructed. What we call communism is a *real, effective* movement, which will destroy the present state of affairs.[3]

During the past ten years, when Marxism has been under careful historical study as well as being subjected to empirical strains in the socialist countries, Soviet heavy periodicals have devoted much space to the problem of alienation. Some articles have divided attention between alienation and existentialism, others have broadened the field to include the problem of freedom, which is inevitably involved in both, and even to deal with such basic questions as the meaning of man and his place in the universe. It is of some significance that these problems are also discussed in popular Soviet publications and that perhaps the most intelligible and meaningful statements are to be found in the *Znaniye* (Knowledge) brochures issued in a series called *Filosofiya* (Philosophy). They are published twice a month in an edition of about 30,000 and sell for fifteen kopecks. This seems to indicate a rather wide spread of Soviet interest in these matters.

One can detect several reasons for the revival of the discussion on alienation. The principle one is, of course, the post-Stalin relaxation of controls on research and expression which, even though minimal, has liberated much thinking hitherto inhibited or kept within intimate groups. Feeding this urge to study and to state one's findings has been the increasing availability of non-Soviet documentation made available in various forms: foreign books and periodicals, radio broadcasts in Russian and other Soviet languages, and formal exchanges of persons, films, music, theatre, and also industrial products. The Soviet authorities do not, however, place this information at the disposal of all citizens. Quite the contrary, non-socialist publications from abroad are only accessible in a restricted number of library reading rooms, except in the case of technical literature and matter which in itself is critical of the Western world. Nevertheless, substantial information does get spread around.

This combination of relaxation and control has had the inevitable effect—dialectically, one might say—of leading to fresh scrutiny of many hitherto sacrosanct Marxist principles and practices. This process has drawn the attention of journalists and scholars the world over and some of them have deduced false premises or a withering away of the Marxist ideological superstructure, along with changes in economic and political practices. Quite naturally Soviet philosophers have

---

[3] *Ibid.*, p. 96.

been alert to such ideas. The sharp reaction by Oizerman[4] to the book *Etudes sur Marx et Hegel* (Paris, 1955) by the French existentialist, J. Hyppolite, reveals where the shoe pinches. Oizerman quotes Hyppolite as saying: "The Hegelian and Feuerbachian idea of alienation constitutes the source of Marx's philosophical thought," and continues:

> This leads to the conclusion that although Marx wrote the four volumes of *Das Kapital*, he did not provide an authentic economic and historical foundation for socialism: his proposition regarding the inevitability of transition from the antagonistic capitalist system to a classless society is, in effect, only a doctrine concerning the development and overcoming of alienation, which goes back to Hegel and Feuerbach, and in the opinion of some (A. Meyer and M. A. Lange) to romantic historiography and even to the Christian teaching of the Fall and the advent of a messiah (according to the well-known French personalist E. Mounier.)[5]

Oizerman goes on: "Such an interpretation, or rather perversion of Marxism, tries in a most direct manner to show that Marxism in its ideological essence and by its origin does not have a direct relation to the liberation movement of the working class."[6] From these quotations it is evident that the study of alienation has threatened to discount the basic socio-economic objectives of Marxism and is no mere peripheral criticism: it raises fundamental questions which concern the whole of Marx-Engels-Lenin philosophy and practice. In order to deal with these questions appropriately in this paper, we need a base line from which to start. For this purpose let me give an amateur summary of the traditional Marxist position: The origin and basis of everything in the universe is matter-in-motion leading to change. There is no supernatural, no metaphysics, no God. Quantitative change is followed by qualitative change—gas to solid to animation to consciousness to social forms. Knowledge is the reflection in the human mind of the real world of matter-in-motion. Mind and matter are inseparable, and together they constitute a refutation of idealism. Mind-matter in joint action create the products of labour. The nature of man is determined by the characteristics of his society, by the relationships in the process of production. Under the capitalist system, part of the product is alienated from the producer. The overcoming of such alienation is possible only by class-consciousness, revolution, universalizing both the problem and the cure. The Party scientifically defines and directs the progress of production, class-consciousness and class war. The Party cannot err; it recognizes change in the mode of expression but not in the essence of Marxist doctrine. Since the Party is scientifically right, its decisions are ethically moral.

With due apology for errors and omissions in this formulation, may we not consider that these propositions constitute the bed-rock foundations on which the monolith of the Soviet Marxist system has been built. Therefore, a basic

---

[4] T. I. Oizerman, *Problema otchuzhdeniya i burzhuaznaya legenda o Marksizme; Filosofiya, II Seriya* (The Problem of Alienation and the Bourgeois Legend about Marxism. Philosophy, Series II), Nos. 19—20, Moscow, 1965.

[5] *Ibid.*, p. 17.

[6] *Ibid.*

tactic, for Marxists is to resist any attack upon or attempted erosion of the mono-lith at any point, whether from inside or from without. On the other hand, the very novely and ambitiousness of the Marxist system lead to doubt, question and resistance to it. This is the mood currently characterizing intellectuals in the Soviet Union today. Warnings are issued and punitive measures are taken against them under charges of infraction of law, corruption of mind and morals, endan-gering the public order, besmirching the international image of Marxism, and hindering the achievement of world revolution.

Lacking a sense of humour, for humour is subjective, not scientifically objec-tive, while at the same time being subjective in their objectivity, Party theoreti-cians and some of the administrators take mortal offence at a jibe at the Kom-somol, or at resistance to the personality cult, or spoofing of the bureaucracy. The border-line between self-criticism, which is welcomed, and real criticism, which is condemned, is very fine. Since the Soviet system provides for analysis, development and defence of its operations, but not for criticism of its basic doctrines, Party chiefs at times show leniency with criticism, so long as it is kept within the family. Their ire rises when outsiders get involved. But the very fact of outside intervention tends to soften the Party's indictment of Soviet critics, leading them to lay the blame on foreign influence rather than on internal natural causes. The Party blasts capitalist poisoners of the minds of good Soviet citizens. In this way it can give a lesson to erring citizens by whipping the scapegoat screaming in the capitalist desert.

The Mexico City Conference of Philosophers, in 1963, did not inaugurate the current philosophical debate, but it did provide a springboard for Soviet attacks on the Western philosophers who are charged with corrupting Soviet intellectuals. An article in *Kommunist*, No. 2, 1965, asserted that the Soviet dele-gates at Mexico City had vanquished all contenders in the philosophical field, except those who fought under the banner of religion. Even though the battle was won, therefore, the war is still on. It is being waged on a broad front in the Soviet Union. The more commonplace religious topics are handled in *Nauka i religiya* (Science and Religion) and in a vast number of books and pamphlets on the subject. The philosophers, on the other hand, currently pick up the quarrel with religion by dealing with the more abstract problems of human freedom, the meaning of life and of man in society, as they appear in existential writers, Chris-tians or non-Christians, in other countries.

Kierkegaard, Heidegger, Jaspers, Hyppolite and Sartre have been analyzed in great detail. Barth, Brunner, Niebuhr and Tillich receive honourable mention, and Martin Luther King was given a long article in *Problems of Philosophy*.[7] Exiled Russian writers in Paris, especially Frank, Bulgakoff and Berdyaev, are constantly being referred to and refuted, and it would appear that many of their works are well-known and influential in the Soviet Union. Marxists find a certain affinity with existentialist writers, since both groups tend to develop ideas and express

---

[7] *Voprosy filosofii*, No. 7, 1965, pp. 114—25.

16

themselves in couplets or contradictions and, what is more important, both find alienation to be a question of prime importance.

I. S. Narsky, writing in *Higher School Scientific Reports, Philosophical Science*, on "The Problem of Alienation in Existentialism and Religion,"[8] makes an exhaustive analysis of the writings of Heidegger and Jaspers, tracing back their lines of thinking to Feuerbach, Hegel and Kant. He first takes Heidegger's book, *Nietzsche* (Berlin, 1961): "Heidegger interprets nihilism as an historical process which to the greatest degree devaluates all human culture, leading to its emptying, i.e., analogous to the manner in which other bourgeois philosophers describe the process of increasing universal alienation. 'Alienation' and 'value' appear in this interpretation to be diametrically opposite categories."

After discussing the "two types of nihilism and two aspects of existentialism" in Nietzsche, the author comments further:

> The mystery of human life is described in existentialist psychology as the absurdity of the appearance of man on earth....For this "mystery" there is a "dual exit." If a man does not know this, his meeting with the fact of the absurdity of existence leads to a mental break-up, and almost to a schizophrenia of his dismembered parts. There arises a third alienation of existence, also quite special but also the most disastrous type of break-up, viz., the passive truth of despair, filling man with fear and dread, and thereby beating him down.[9]

Then follows a reference to man's efforts to regain balance by undertaking ordinary daily duties, "trying to forget the nightmare of metaphysical collision." Narsky says that Heidegger's characterization of this "everydayness" is "human depersonalization," whereas the "religious existentialist Jaspers calls it an effort to retreat into the 'shell' of self-deception." He feels that Sartre leads up to absurdity in this sentence which he quotes from *Critique de la Raison Dialectique* : "And exactly in the concrete and intermediary connection of one factor with another (*l'agent a l'autre*), through the intermediary of an object (thing), and of that object through the intermediary of another, we find the basis for all sorts of alienation."

Narsky's comment is as follows: "In the imagination of the existentialists, everydayness presumably composes, tranquilizes the person, but by this very fact it drags out of him all that is authentically human, alienates him in a nonauthentic world....Man comes close to being a beast or a machine, it kills individuality in him, levels him off and destroys his personality."[10]

The Christian doctrine of the fall into sin, i.e., fatal alienation from God through the curiosity of Adam and Eve, the change from innocence to guilt, depicts according to Narsky, "the primary quality of man's earthly nature, the paradisical curiosity of ignorance was transformed into earthly thirst for pleasure, a striving for possessions. Because of increasing thirst and craving, man constantly alienates himself in sinful acts...." He writes that "modern neo-Thomists eagerly transform the Biblical myth regarding the beginning of man's existence

---

[8] *Nauchniye doklady vysshey shkoly ; filosofskiye nauki*, No. 1, Moscow, 1966.

[9] *Ibid.*, p. 63.

[10] *Ibid.*, p. 64.

into the terminology of alienation. (See J. Hommes, *Zweispältiges Dasein*, Freiburg, 1953)." His final comment is this: "Existentialism as such does not reject social activity, but by its teaching of the basic futility (alienation) of any results of such activity, it fulfills exactly this ideological mission, which is bourgeois in essence."[11]

Is the opposition of Marxists to the existentialists based in part on the affinity of their respective docrines? The teaching of Marx regarding the absolute nature of the relationship of man to matter, of human cognition to that which the mind reflects, the bond between society and the laws of nature and of social development—all this comes close to the existentialist concept that what is, is. The distinction between Marxism and the existentialists arises at the point where an intellectual and moral conclusion is to be reached. Existentialists tend to despair; Marxists are prone to thrill.

At another point they are either in sharp contradiction or in close approximation, viz., in regard to human personality and freedom. Existentialists concentrate on these things. Their great aspiration is for freedom from any and all sorts of laws and controls, because for them the individual personality cannot be fully itself if limited by restrictions or compulsions. For them, alienation is the break-up and separation of part of an individual's personality in response to the demands of society's laws. Hence comes a revolt, an effort to break the bonds with society, and thereby to achieve uninhibited, completely self-directed thinking and acting.

Here we see how futility arises, expressed in terms relevant to the nihilism of Nietzsche, the moodiness of Sartre, the unresolved contradictions of Jaspers and Heidegger. The Marxists claim that the real answer is easily found in the natural integrality of individual and society. Instead of rejecting society, as the existentialists do, Marxism gives it primary place, in fact the generating place, for the reason that society forms man and creates his personality. All that is needed is for man to realize this, to look about him, and enjoy the freedom which society makes possible—production of goods, making them available for use or consumption, protection against fear and disease, and the pleasures of company.

In another of these popular Soviet philosophical brochures, *The Problem of Man*, the author gives his explanation of alienation:

> Relationships between people under capitalism take the form of relationships between things, the products of labour. Although the worker is no longer the property of the master, yet he continues to be dependent upon him by reason of economic necessity. Even though unseen, the real power of capital hangs over the person. The working capacity of a man also becomes goods.... This domination over the activity of persons and the product of their activity is commonly called the alienation of man, i.e., the domination of elemental social forces over man.[12]

It would seem that the liquidation of capitalism in the Soviet Union must have eliminated the problem of alienation. And yet they have SMOG in Moscow.

---

[11] *Ibid.*, p. 71.

[12] A. G. Myslivchenko, *Problema cheloveka; Filosofiya*, Series II, Moscow, 1965, p. 5.

These are the initial letters of the Russian words *smyelost, mysli, obraz, glubina* (boldness, thought, image, depth). According to *Komsomolskaya pravda*, (June 20, 1965) this group states that "the basic method of expression for Smogists is split-personality, a twilight condition of the soul, existential thinking." These young people can hardly be said to have a normal, healthy, integrated personality.

A key element in all of this is productive labour and attitude toward it. People anywhere whose philosophy is freedom *from* everything seem to abhor work. This is another reason why Soviet law is exceptionally severe on "parasites," those who do not wish to work. Society generally, whether communist or capitalist, recognizes the right to work as one of the greatest of freedoms. But here a distinction must be drawn. In communist society productive labour is not only a right but an obligation; Marxists repeat, but without Biblical reference, the phrase, "he who does not work shall not eat." In planned society, where production and distribution of goods conform to this Marxist philosophy, the practical effect is that of a choice between work or self-extinction. Nevertheless labour does not play a large part in the recent discussion of alienation in the Soviet press, perhaps because a man's work is subsumed under the discussions of the role of the individual in society.

We have referred to the careful consideration given to freedom and personality as philosophical concepts. These concepts assume ethical values, as they express themselves in daily life. The Marxist position on ethics is plainly stated: moral law is inherent in the process of production, from which human life and relationships proceed. Answering religion, Marxism says that there is no existence apart from matter-in-motion, therefore no supernatural, and no God or gods to make moral law. Theoretically this ends the matter, yet the subject of religion and the religious basis for ethics appear often in the Soviet press. Marxism says that the existentialist is wrong in pitting himself against society: join the crowd and you will forget your woes. Nevertheless, quite a lot of critical attention is given to those, whether religious or not, who would put the stamp of moral legitimacy on whatever society at a given period finds congenial. Especially condemned are the young people who feel ostracized if they do not follow "the mode"—such as acquiring a black market copy of Kafka.[13] A distinction is here made between Marxist society, on the one hand, which by virtue of its inner relationship with matter-in-motion reflects and confirms only that which is ethically right, and capitalist society on the other which, they say, is essentially a contradiction of that which is right. Capitalist society is a product of the alienation of man from himself. This process of alienation destroys the inner harmony of matter-in-motion, and is therefore ethically wrong by nature's own standards, not by "divine law."

Current Soviet literature on this subject takes account of the tendency in the West to "ascribe a special mystical power to technology," and for "bourgeois philosophers" to try to "protect personality against the 'demonic' impact of technics." Jaspers is quoted (*Die geistige Situation der Zeit*, Berlin, 1960) as saying

---

[13] *Molodoy kommunist*, No. 1, 1966.

that the operating worker is transformed into a part of the machine; "in order to exist, everyone must put forth his maximum strength; anxiety and the compulsion to work harder grow, it is known that the one who falls behind is lost, after the age of forty he feels thrown overboard."[14] Automation, computers, cybernetics, all enter into this discussion. A curious development in Marxist thought may be mentioned here. In the *Kratky filosofsky slovar* (Short Philosophical Dictionary), 1952 edition, the term cybernetics was referred to as a "false science," whereas in 1965 there are whole faculties devoted to its study. It is here charged that under capitalism there is alienation not only of the product of work but of the personality of the worker, and a man who has thus lost his personality has also lost the basis of moral rights inherent in his manhood.

We shall later on venture to respond to this analysis, but need first to go more deeply into the communist position. In the above-quoted brochure, *The Problem of Man*, Myslivchenko writes, "thus the individual, taken anthropologically, is torn away from his social foundations. Whatever is social is considered inimical to man, sharply contradictory to anthropological man, who, incidentally, is treated not on the rational scientific plane but irrationally, subjectively." Consideration of the possibility of a fundamental change in the nature of man, anthropologically, leads the author to refer to Freud, who is quoted as saying, "man of prehistoric epochs, unchanged, continues to live in our sub-consciousness." Some paragraphs tell of the Freudian emphasis on sex, and then Simone de Beauvoir is quoted as identifying anthropological man with sex: "the happiness of man is not in God, patriotism, beauty, justice, love, family, friendship, work. Man's happiness is in sex, because man and sex are identical." The author comments that "the true meaning of the existence of man has been ignored."

When Myslivchenko deals with the Western personalist philosophy, religion again appears: "The capacity of a personality to have relationships with others is interpreted in a religious spirit. They hold that the highest form of 'other' is God, and that man's personality derives from the personality of God....Another's personality (thou) is connected with mine (I) simply because it is spiritually connected with the same God as mine." Further, neo-Thomists are given nearly a page, in which credit is given to them for criticizing the "extreme subjectivism of existential 'absolute' freedom." The Thomistic distinction between two types of freedom, (1) freedom of the will and (2) autonomous freedom, is noted. The first is related to earthly desires, and leads to sin; the second is on a higher plane, enables man to put a brake on desire, to seek happiness of non-material nature. "Happiness, according to the neo-Thomists, consists in love of God and efforts to draw near to him." The Marxist conclusion is that the rejection of earthly joys "pours ascetic water on the propagandistic mills of the exploiting classes." Here is a return to the original Marxist theory of alienation, a socio-economic condition which can be overcome only by world-wide class struggle.

There is a return to this basic theme also in Oizerman's *The Problem of Alienation and the Bourgeois Legend about Marxism*. Burgelin is quoted as saying that

---

[14] A. G. Myslivchenko, *op. cit.*, p. 9.

Marxists "have perverted the great Christian ideas, and we do not know whither they are calling mankind. Incidentally they have been able to seize the place which our faithlessness has left vacant." But the Marxists refute every suggestion that their theories have anything to do, historically or philosophically, with religious concepts regarding man, his personality or his freedom; "The essence of the Marx-Lenin scientific approach to the question of personality, of the individual, consists simply in an analysis of the social nature of the individual, his social conditioning and his relationship to social elements." They hold that bourgeois philosophers are stupid, turning to illusory philosophies detached from reality (material existence) and arriving only at the conclusion that "the contradictions in human life are irreconcilable, that life is tragedy, that scientific technical progress presents a fatal threat to mankind."[15] We pause to remark that one has only to read the last third of the leading article in almost any issue of *Pravda* to find the same sort of dismal analysis, but directed toward the people who are unfaithfully or listlessly carrying out the communist programme. The Party is always fully convinced of the correctness of the programme itself and of the theory behind it.

The fundamental problem in both Marxist and non-Marxist society is man, his relationship to nature, his situation in the world of automation, cybernetics and space, and his relationship to other men. We have tried to be fair in drawing upon Marxist writings in order to set forth their views on this problem. In their literature, however, we find either a flat negation or a scornful rejection of certain elements which, in our opinion, need more favourable consideration, such as the following: (1) the normal resilience of most of the people in any society, enabling them to withstand or overcome alienation, whether caused by their own frailty, the tensions of Western sophistication or the pressures of Marxist self-assumed omniscience; (2) the anthropological normalcy of the concept of the supernatural, of God and of spiritual power; (3) the reasonableness of expecting that moral concepts shall be found not *a priori* in a social philosophy or in existential practice, but in the treasury of deeper human experience, including man's experience of relationship with ultimate good.

Whether we think of alienation in the economic terminology of Karl Marx, detachment of part of the self in the form of the product of labour, or in the ethical sense of St. Paul, "what I would I do not, and what I would not, that I do," or as the sub-consciousness of Freud, or the pessimism of Jaspers—we get the impression that all the world is crazy, or nearly so. But then we look about us, our family, school, office, factory or on the street, and we have to say that most of us seem normal. Perhaps alienation is a latent factor, present in one aspect or another in every one of us, by virtue of the parallel existence of freedom and its denial. It is normal for man and society to pass through fluctuations, to win and to lose, to feel free and to feel cramped. The error of Marxism is to hold that these contradictions can be completely overcome in communist society. Giving the Marxist credit for effort, he is still not at the head of the class. Similarly the anti-Marxists have no grounds for complacency. The "leading cadres" in both

---

[15] T. I. Oizerman, *op. cit.*, pp. 55, 58.

societies can be thankful that most of the people are gifted with the capacity for adjustment and the habit of keeping their heads.

Our second point above aims to record another error which some Marxist theoreticians have admitted, albeit grudgingly. Statistics presented at the colloquium in Jena, East Germany, in June, 1965, indicate a considerable falling off of religious belief and habits. Interestingly enough, Marxist and non-Marxist countries come out about the same. This is the point we wish to make, that the sense of the presence and action of God is not subject to localization by social-economic systems. We would not venture to say that Marx, Lenin and the Leninists were not convinced and authentic atheists. We do say that Marx and Engels arrived at their pivotal authentic positions by a process of philosophical conflict, an intellectual *tour de force*, in which they put a fence around the field of their own mental processes and left God outside. Some thinkers have lived within this stockade but, while there, by using the same Marxist processes of logical thought, have deduced the existence of the supernatural and the necessity of His presence for the better regulation of human life. Reference is not only to the Russian ex-Marxist thinkers such as Berdyaev and Bulgakoff, but to some Westerners as well. St. Augustine was expressing the deeper concern of man of all times and places when he said, "my soul is distraught until it find its rest in Thee."

The problem of evil is the opposite of the joy of the good. Some concentrate on evil and its eradication, others on the good and its establishment. These things go together. Marxist doctrine seems to hold that it has discovered the roots of evil, or rather that it has two roots. First is the capitalist system with its perpetuation of alienation of the product of labour; class struggle and universal communist rule will remove this root. Second is the concept of God, of the supernatural, which, they say, capitalistic exploiters use to stupefy the proletariat. Theoretically this second root will wither and disappear as the first is eradicated.

Here is a strange situation. Many of the "goods" in communism come straight out of the age-old teachings of religion, Jewish, Christian, Muslim or Buddhist. Or do they? Is it a case of "any resemblance is wholly incidental?" The dilemma now facing Marxist philosophers is a pragmatic one. Not only the old but many of the young in communist countries are pointing to these ancient sources for moral law. Some publicly reveal a mysticism quite contrary to the pure intellectualism (matter-in-motion) of a true communist. What is Yevtushenko's passionate cry, "Double, triple the guard!" but a sense of a mystical evil present in the world?

The question naturally arises as to how religious people in the Soviet Union deal with the problem of alienation, and in general with the philosophy of Marx-Engels-Lenin. One looks in vain for relevant items in the *Zhurnal Moskovskoy Patriarkhii* (Journal of the Moscow Patriarchate) or in the *Bratsky vestnik* (Brotherly Messenger) of the Union of Evangelical Christian Baptists. Neither Orthodox nor Baptists publish books or pamphlets of apologetic type. This would seem to indicate a complete separation not only of Church and state but of religion and life. However, some objective circumstances may be noted. The two theological academies and the three seminaries concentrate on providing knowledge of biblical and patristic character. They have no seminars, workshops or open discussions, and produce no dissertations on social theory or on such problems as alienation. Their epistemology stresses spiritual revelation rather than sensory knowledge, and omits reference to the Marxist "reflect" principle.

Matters of public concern do enter into the thinking and life of the churches, and public expression on these matters appears almost exclusively in connection with "peace" meetings. Yet the historical and even ontological relation between church and world is occasionally expressed, as in the following excerpts from the address of Metropolitan Nikodim on October 28, 1965,[16] at the consecration of Nikolai as Bishop of Tikhvin: "Knowing the organic connection between faith and life, being a lamp in the world, standing high on the pillar, and to the same purpose appeal to your fellow pastors and to all who are faithful to Christ.... A bishop 'must not only be pure, worthy of such great service, but very wise and experienced in many things, acquainted with the affairs of the world no less than those in the world who turn to him,' in the words of St. John Chrysostom."

The significance of the quotation from St. John Chrysostom will not have been lost on hearers or readers, for they know that Chrysostom was a great fighter for social justice and in fact died on the road to exile in the year 407.

Those of us who have personal contact with the Orthodox Church in the Soviet Union know that some of the clergy and laity read and discuss philosophy and psychology as well as church-state affairs. Father Paul Florensky, priest and physicist, who died in a Soviet prison; Boris Vyacheslavtsev, whose *Philosophy of Transfigured Eros*[17] draws heavily on Hegel and Fichte; and Nicholas Berdyaev, whose personal path led him through Marxism to Christ, are among their intellectual guides. Berdyaev's philosophy of creativity, of man's participation in God's continuing work of creation, helps to meet the Marxist matter-in-motion doctrine; and his many other writings touch upon both the problems of cognition and of man in society.

Under existing conditions, when even secular poets and novelists who call themselves Marxists are restrained or punished for critical works, it is not unnatural that Christians, already suspect, should restrain themselves and be like the three Oriental monkeys: see nothing, hear nothing, say nothing.

The one strong point on which the Orthodox and other religious people stand, and on which the life of their churches persists, is their experience of the presence of God. Marxists consider this experience, if it exists, as being subjective, lacking any possibility of scientific proof, and therefore having no place in communist society. Perhaps the question is this: who is alienated from whom? The proletariat from its product, with solution in class-struggle, or individual men from God, with solution in Christ—the way, the truth and the life.

---

[16] *Zhurnal Moskovskoy Patriarkhii*, No. 11, Moscow, 1965.

[17] B. P. Vyacheslavtsev, *Filosofiya preobrazhennogo erosa*, YMCA Press, Paris, 1936.

Orthodoxy and the Younger Generation in the USSR

Dmitry Konstantinov

The Orthodox Church is a vital and profound source of the spiritual and intellectual ferment now occurring in the Soviet Union as part of the irreversible process of renewal taking place before our eyes. Despite the fundamental conflict between the dogmas of the Orthodox Church and the values of the Soviet regime, it is the inspiration from religion that pervades much of the urge to attain new spiritual horizons.

Orthodoxy has experienced many vicissitudes over the last half century, and has been bent to the needs of the regime in the latter's religious policy. Yet, in the face of all the pressure and persecution at the hands of the communist authorities, for many decades, and especially under Stalin, the Church remained the only haven of spiritual freedom and the only antithesis to the official materialist philosophy. Christianity, embodied in the Church, is seeping into every strata of Soviet society and is affecting everyone who is not dead in spirit. In one form or another it is stimulating the spiritual awakening of the most disparate groups within this society. Here and there this process comes to a halt and peters out at differing stages of the individual's spiritual and mental development. But sometimes Christian values are transformed into philosophical or political ideas in which the principles of intellectual and political freedom predominate. Notwithstanding its apparently conservative nature, so often commented upon by foreign writers, Orthodoxy is imbued with a spirit of freedom. And although the dogmatic and canonical stability of Orthodoxy protects it from all assaults on its wholeness, the creative spiritual freedom within it bears fruitful results both within the Church and outside it. There is a need to stress this fact, because a widely held opinion asserts that the "conservatism" and "limitedness" of the Church are obstacles preventing Orthodoxy from influencing the Soviet young generation. This is not true; if any impediments do exist, they arise because the young sometimes find it hard to thoroughly understand Orthodoxy in its complexity and diversity.

What are the paths by which young people in the Soviet Union are approaching Orthodoxy? Dealing with the matter ten years ago I arrived at the conclusion that one of the main ways is simply by becoming acquainted with the liturgy at Mass.[1] This is still largely true today, with the only difference that since recently new means of religious education have been made available in the shape of the Scriptures: nowadays religious literature in mimeographed or even printed form is passed from hand to hand, and the works of Russian and Western

---

[1] D. V. Konstantinov, *Pravoslavnaya molodezh v borbe za Tserkov v SSSR* (Orthodox Youth in its Fight for the Church in the USSR), Munich, 1965, Institute for the Study of the USSR, p. 74; "Soviet Youth in its Fight for the Church (1920—1930)," *Vestnik Instituta po izucheniyu istorii i kultury SSSR*, Munich, No. 1 (14), 1955.

religious philosophers are being studied, now that access to them is becoming easier. Religious literature comes in from abroad and even the Moscow Patriarchate manages to print some.

In a recent article on the present position of the Orthodox Church in the USSR, an American journalist compared Orthodoxy in the Soviet Union with an iceberg, only the tip of which shows above the surface.[2] The main part of the religious processes so far remains invisible and therefore only the results are apparent, not the impulse behind them. We have to judge these processes chiefly from what we read in the Soviet press, which almost daily sounds the alarm over religion. A reflection is also to be found in letters received in the West from religious believers, the accounts of those who have visited the Soviet Union, and in the illegal literature produced in the country itself, examples of which find their way abroad. The outside observer is faced with the hard task of analysing this mosaic of information and of piecing together an accurate picture of the situation.

Any examination of the influence of the Orthodox Church over the young generation in the Soviet Union must deal with all the different degrees of commitment to religious faith, beginning with those who are whole-hearted members of the Church and ending with those young people who, although perhaps not practising Christians, are capable of expressing such sentiments as this:

> And the wind has borne away
> So much time.
> Yet Rus is still scattered with little churches
> Waiting for God.[3]

One may next quote the most arresting examples of the way in which youth is being drawn to the Orthodox Church. Over the past few years the Soviet press has been reporting a succession of cases of young people who have fallen under religious influences. There was Valeri, the son of a high Party member, brought up in an anti-religious atmosphere, who joined the Komsomol and studied at the Moscow Physical Culture Institute. Suddenly, however, he began losing interest in his studies, after a short while became completely indifferent to Komsomol activities and submitted two applications, one for permission to leave the Institute, the other to enter a seminary.[4] Unfortunately we cannot know the process which took place within Valeri to engender such a transformation.

"I am through with him," said the wife of a young collective farm worker, Melenti Romanenko, after he decided to enter the priesthood despite her desperate efforts to prevent him from doing so, in which she went as far as to denounce him to the local office of the state security committee. Yet none of the authorities with which Romanenko had to deal, in order to obtain the necessary papers allowing him to leave the farm, made any difficulties, although they could easily have done so. They simply completed the legal formalities without at-

---

[2] *The New York Times*, March 7, 1966.

[3] *Sfinksy*, No. 1, reprinted in *Grani*, Moscow, No. 59, 1965, p. 24.

[4] *Izvestia*, October 14, 1960.

tempting to dissuade the young man from his purpose by means of any atheist arguments. This suggests that they may even have been tacitly in sympathy with or at least not antagonistic to his desire to devote his life to the Church, despite having themselves been brought up in a non-religious atmosphere.[5]

Then there is the case of Vasili Dyukov, a young bricklayer who had just married and settled down with his wife. The harmonious married life was not to last long. Vasili started meeting the local clergy and attending mass at the local Orthodox Church, and within a short time decided to enter a seminary. This was a heavy blow to his wife, who was completely indifferent to religion and did all in her power to prevent her husband from carrying out his intention. In the end he gave up the idea, but was soon drafted for military service, during which, it appears, he still clung to religion.[6]

It had been a long-standing wish of G. Filippovich, a contributor to *Nauka i religiya*, the anti-religious journal, to write a report about a Soviet village where religion has had its day and where, as a result of well-organized propaganda, "religious survivals" had been overcome. In order to gather the necessary material, Filippovich travelled through the Mari ASSR and eventually came to the town of Volzhsk, where he went to see the head of the local branch of the atheist *Znaniye* organization. What ensued is worth quoting verbatim:

> I asked a man I met in the hall where the head of the atheist department was.
>
> He is not in, the comrade answered briefly.
>
> Will he be in today?
>
> No, nor tomorrow either, nor the day after tomorrow. He is studying for his exams.
>
> What for?
>
> For admission to a seminary. He has already submitted his application. "You must be joking," I said. To be quite frank, I felt he must be insulting me. "I am asking you a serious question," I said. "Well, I'm answering you seriously. If you don't believe me, ask comrade Ponomarev, secretary of the town committee on ideology. His office is on the second floor."

Filippovich goes to see the secretary, who confirms what he has been told and says with some embarrassment that it is "a case that can hardly be said to flatter us," and this is the title Filippovich gives to his article.[7]

The religious focus of the town of Orenburg is still the Nikolsky Cathedral, which is not far away from school No. 35. And the Soviet press has something to complain about on this score:

> Peacefully they (the church and the school) stand almost side by side, but in reality, where the spheres of influence of these two focuses clash, a never-ending struggle is taking place for the human soul. The teaching staff at the school is not bad, and our whole way of life aids it in this struggle. And yet it does not always

---

[5] *Ibid.*, May 20, 1961.

[6] *Sovetskaya Rossiya*, June 29, 1962.

[7] *Nauka i religiya*, No. 5, 1964, p. 73.

emerge victorious. Inozemtsev, a pupil at this school, graduated and then went into a seminary. He returned to his home town as a priest. Now he officiates and helps to lure children into church.[8]

Another pupil, Ilya Borodin, after graduating from school No. 34 in Orenburg also took holy orders, although he later left the church.

The fact that all these cases have been reported in the Soviet press is evidence enough that they are not isolated, otherwise so much publicity would not be given to them. To judge by the concern shown by the authorities, the people who cherish the desire to devote their lives to the Church come from all walks of life, belong to all age groups and are clearly quite numerous. In the mid-1950's, for instance, there were eight seminaries and two ecclesiastical academies in the USSR, but the number of applicants for admission was far higher than the number of vacant places. Each seminary had an average of 2,000 students annually, not counting those taking evening courses. It is also reported that there was no lack of girls ready and willing to marry newly-ordained priests.[9]

The Soviet press has ceased to claim that only old people go to church, and that it is old women who predominate. It is true that women and the elderly of both sexes do form a large part of congregations in churches in the Soviet Union, but this is the case in the West as well, and even in pre-revolutionary Russia there were usually few young people and men at services. One reason is that women the world over are much more punctilious in observance of religious rites than men. In the Soviet Union there is an additional factor accounting for the large number of women attending church: it is safer for a woman to perform religious devotions than for a man when the state is hostile to religious observance and victimization may result at a man's place of work, as happens in the Soviet Union if someone is found to be a regular church-goer. Some excuse may even be found for sacking such a person. Also, more indulgence is shown to women who display "ideological immaturity" by going to church.

In the last few years, however, the proportion of young people attending Mass has increased, and this is being admitted by the authorities. A photograph appeared in the press showing a group of believers during Easter Service, waiting for the consecration of cakes and *paskha* (a sweet cream-cheese confection traditionally eaten at Easter).[10] The congregation included children, teen-agers, and young girls and women hardly over 30 years of age. Another photograph showed an 18-year old pilgrim carrying a cross. The accompanying article displayed a frankness that marked a new departure in the official approach, which had hitherto tried to play down this participation by the young. The author is writing about the town of Tambov:

> I was told by local atheists: "Only old people go to church. We went to church during Lent in order to see for ourselves. And you too can go and see for yourself..."
> The following Sunday I went and saw for myself. The Pokrovsky cathedral com-

[8] *Izvestia*, November 27, 1965.

[9] *Grani*, No. 48, 1960, pp. 213—236.

[10] *Nauka i religiya*, No. 12, 1965, p. 2.

prises two churches... It has a long one-storey wing on one side where babies are christened and funeral services held, etc. All this is done by six priests.

The cathedral priests deserve credit for working without bureaucracy or formalism. That Sunday morning they celebrated mass three times, heard confessions, held a memorial service for the souls of the dead, administered the sacrament to those who had just adopted the Orthodox faith, and gave the Eucharist to those thirsting for the body and blood of Christ. The same morning one priest was christening babies in the side wing, another was holding funeral services in the cemetery, and still another was doing his rounds "on call" in his car.

The church-yard was overcrowded. There were old men and women, as expected by the atheists. There were also persons who had not been foreseen. Against the background of fresh green foliage and the black garments of the pilgrims stood out the whiteness of the babies' quilts. There was also a quiet, jostling crowd of small boys and girls with little multicoloured bows in their plaits, their mouths agape with wonder. These young boys and girls who had just been made "acquainted with Orthodoxy" had not been foreseen in any atheist plans either, nor had their godparents of Komsomol age or slightly older, but completely ignorant of church matters. They are kindly instructed by old women, but not by those backward grandmothers whom the atheists gave up as hopeless a long time ago.

...Between the early and late Mass a queue of people formed in front of the confessional, waiting to repent of their sins. There again we see old women as foreseen by the plan, including, however, pupils of the first few grades.[11]

There is, however, still a law on the Soviet statute book that forbids children and teen-agers under 18 to attend Mass. An editorial to Kostyukov's article states mournfully: "Unfortunately, the facts cited above are not only typical of Tambov."

Another article describes church life in Georgia, and refers in particular to the Cathedral of Mtskheta:

The Mtskheta Cathedral. The marriage service of a young couple is being celebrated with great pomp. The groom, Merab Vasholomidze, a junior staff member in an important ideological establishment, namely, the Institute of Philosophy, had his civil marriage performed at a registry office, and then decided to consolidate it by means of a ceremony in church...

...There were another one and a half hours to go before the all-night service, but the bells were already calling for service. An aged priest placed one child after the other into the font with a haste ill befitting his age, while a young priest of the Russian Orthodox Church, aged about 30, was celebrating mass in the right nave of the church. The relatively small space was crowded with devout worshippers. Here too, the number of young people was not small.[12]

And another correspondent writes that "something is wrong" in the village of Ternov in Voronezh Oblast: "The clergymen have built a rather strong nest here. It happens that young people attend church service. A cunning, ingenious priest is doing his duty, christening babies, marrying young couples."[13] The

[11] Ibid., pp. 32–34.
[12] Ibid., No. 5, 1963, pp. 71–72.
[13] Komsomolskaya pravda, March 26, 1963.

correspondent adds that the priest has started cooperating with the local Komsomol. A report on religious life in the town of Kentau in the Chimkent Oblast of Kazakhstan asks: "And who are these believers? They include grey-bearded, aged men, but also still very young people."[14] Elsewhere in the press we find a description of the Pskovo-Pechersky Monastery just before the beginning of the evening service: "The janitor at the gate, our old friend Vasili, a lay-brother who had come to work at the holy cloister from Novgorod, is hardly capable of keeping off the masses of people."[15] Reference is specifically made not to "masses of old women and children" but to "masses of people." A quotation from an article written by the Soviet writer Valeri Tarsis, who recently came to live in the West, is an apt commentary:

> Despite atheist propaganda, the number of believers has been growing like flowers after a good spring shower. Last year, on the eve of Easter, my friend and I took a cab and visited ten Moscow churches. This was on Good Friday, and I was happy to see in front of every church long queues of believers holding white bags with *kulich* and *paskha* which they had brought along for consecration. And it was even more delightful to see the faces of numerous young girls among the crowd of believers, amounting on the average to up to 5,000 people. The school-girls had put on their white Sunday aprons, and I noticed that the crowds were considerably larger than in 1963 when I also visited our churches.[16]

However, the conditions under which the rising generation comes to join the Orthodox Church are still more interesting than the above evidence testifying to participation by young people in religious ceremonies. The following are excerpts from the numerous reports on the subject that have been appearing in Soviet anti-religious literature. For example, in an article entitled "Encounters in Stavropol" M. G. Mikhailov writes:

> I asked Ye. R. Androsova about her education. "High school. Then I attended the Stavropol Pedagogical Institute," adding with a smile, "They fired me from the institute—upon my own request."[17]

The article reveals that the reason why the girl was dismissed was that she had not made a secret of her religious feelings. And Androsova referred to her girl friends, who are also true believers:

> I am not the only one. The same thing happened the year before last to Nina Ivleva at the agricultural institute, who is a Baptist. Valya Podgaiskaya had to leave the pedagogical institute. First we were grieved, but then we understood: everything God does is for the best.[18]

The same periodical carries an article about a carpenter, Yevdokim Morgachev, whom the workers at the Urban Foodstuffs Organization had elected to

---

[14] *Kazakhstanskaya pravda*, November 4, 1965.

[15] *Sovetskaya Rossiya*, November 18, 1964.

[16] *Posev*, Frankfurt, February 25, 1966.

[17] *Nauka i religiya*, No. 4, 1965.

[18] *Vestnik russkogo studencheskogo khristianskogo dvizheniya*, (Bulletin of the Russian Student Christian Movement), Paris-New York, No. 78, 1965, p. 32.

their trade-union committee, but whom the management refused to approve as a member because he was a believer. One of the not infrequent cases is cited, too, of the dismissal of a gifted girl Komsomol member. She was expelled from university because she had studied the Bible and become a believer.[19] Another girl, fifteen year-old Lyudmilla L., a student at the Tyumen School of Commerce, started attending an Orthodox Church and eventually turned wholly to religion, which affected not so much her studies as her general conduct and attitude towards all kinds of social activities. After it was found out that she had joined the Church, Lyudmilla was deprived of her only means of existence, her scholarship, and forced to leave school. When faced with the alternative of choosing between the Church and her scholarship, Lyudmilla decided in favour of the former. The newspaper claims that now she stands on the steps of the church with hand outstreched for alms.[20]

Viktor Lebedev, a young lorry driver from the town of Uren in the Urals, joined the Orthodox Church and wanted to enter a monastery but could not do so, since he was married. So he became a missionary and proved to be successful in his work, because he is reported as having "followers." The authorities intervened to put a stop to his activities. He was classed as a "parasite" and sentenced to exile in a "remote region of the republic." However, before the order could be carried out Viktor left the town of Uren and disappeared without trace.[21]

It may be seen from the Soviet press that despite the antireligious propaganda conducted by the Party, Orthodoxy remains an "infectious threat" to youth in the eyes of the authorities. In addition to the cases cited above, publicity has been given to a lorry-driver in Omsk Oblast named Sergei Kozodoyenko, who adopted the Orthodox faith at the age of 35, and of a girl who came to believe in God after attending Mass.[22] Many of these young believers startle the authorities by their readiness to make sacrifices, their heroic attitude and extraordinary perseverance in their determination to cling to their faith. The case of young Anna Skorik, as reported in the press, showed an endless series of persecutions for the sole reason that she was a believer. Since her childhood Anna had been closely connected with the Church and had managed to remain faithful to it despite all the humiliations that the "young fanatic," as she is called, had to suffer at school. She still would not give way even when every employer refused to give her a job, when her sister was dismissed from her place of work and when the order came for her to leave her home town, followed by legal proceedings against her for organizing "illegal prayer meetings." Neither Anna Skorik nor any of the other youngsters whose cases have been quoted above, and many others like them, can count on any support from the Church in their efforts to resist pressure from the authorities. The Church is in no position to render such aid. Nevertheless, both the young generation and those of mature age are fearless in the face of repressions.

---

[19] *Literaturnaya gazeta*, October 20, 1962.
[20] *Sovetskaya Rossiya*, September 27, 1962.
[21] *Ibid.*, June 29, 1962.
[22] *Selskaya zhizn*, June 28, 1962.

A priest belonging to the catacomb church in Tekeli, Kazakhstan, who was discovered and sentenced to five years' imprisonment was only 34 years of age.[23]

The open observance of such Church rites as marriage ceremonies, baptism, etc., over which the Soviet press has repeatedly expressed great concern, must also be mentioned. Marriage in church has become quite popular among Soviet young people, and even among Komsomol members. Komsomol member Valentina Khvorova in the village of Selezni in Tambov Oblast, and Aleksei Mukin from the neighbouring village of Lysye Gory were married at an Orthodox church, and so was the Komsomol secretary, Masha Pudovkina, also from the same village. Both Khvorova and Pudovkina were expelled from the Komsomol shortly after. The correspondent reporting on this mentions that there are no churches functioning in this particular rural region, and so young couples wishing to get married travel to other areas where the churches have not been closed, and especially to the town of Tambov.[24] In Volsk, for instance, 10 couples were married in church and 206 babies christened in 1961, and in 1962 the figures had risen to 59 and 1,795 respectively.[25]

Any discussion of religious activities in the Soviet Union should include reference to the problem regarding children. As mentioned above, the Soviet government passed a law in 1962 forbidding minors to enter an Orthodox church. Christening and receiving the Eucharist is allowed only in the case of babies under 18 months and this only if the names of the parents, godparents, and other persons participating in the ceremony are registered with the authorities. These governmental measures were intended to prevent younger age-groups from following in the footsteps of that part of the rising generation which has adopted Orthodoxy.

It was stated in the Soviet press in 1964 that approximately 500 miners in the town of Tekeli went to the Orthodox church of Taldy-Kurgan in order to have their children christened there, because apparently there was no longer a church in Tekeli. This was a rather dangerous venture in view of the compulsory registration of the parents, introduced in order that measures could be taken against the latter. According to the same press report: "the young wives of two lorry-drivers in Taldy-Kurgan had their babies christened in the customary way....And after her husband divorced her, a certain Elvira Kim made haste to find consolation in church by having her daughter Galya baptised."[26] But baptism is not confined to babes in arms: Lyda Sh., a trained nurse said to be an outstanding worker and Komsomol member, was christened at the age of 20 and then married in church.[27] These are only a few examples but they all testify to the fact that the public as a whole is in favour of baptism.[28]

---

[23] *Kazakhstanskaya pravda*, February 17, 1963.

[24] *Komsomolskaya pravda*, June 6, 1963.

[25] *Krokodil*, No. 16, 1963.

[26] *Kazakhstanskaya pravda*, March 12, 1965.

[27] *Komsomolskaya pravda*, June 6, 1963.

[28] D. Konstantinov, "The Atheist Howl," *Russko-Amerikansky pravoslavny vestnik*, New York, No. 10, 1965, pp. 155—157.

31

Another effort to combat religious upbringing was the formation of numerous state-run boarding schools to which the children of parents with religious beliefs were sent. Over the last few years there has been a wave of legal proceedings in the Soviet Union against parents who bring up their children as Christians. The object of these measures has been to remove such children from the "unhealthy influence" of their homes and place them in state boarding schools. Cases also occur in which one parent wishes the offspring to be reared in a religious atmosphere, while the other does not. When matters end up in the divorce court it is the state that steps in to order the removal of a child from the care of a religiously-inclined parent. These problems also find their reflection on the pages of the press. For example, the wife of Guards Captain Valentin Vasilyevich B. was awarded custody of their son Yura after her husband divorced her. She, in turn, passed him on to her parents in order to have him brought up as an Orthodox Christian. The grandmother started rearing the child according to strict religious rules, and even held prayer meetings in her own flat because the local church had been closed. The captain tried to change matters by submitting a complaint to the newspapers. He also wrote two letters to his former wife about the religious education of his child. The answer to the first one was: "You shall not get the child. It is no business of yours where he is being brought up," and to the second, which mentioned the religious services held in grandmother's flat: "Do not oppose prayers at home. If you do not like them, clear out."[29]

Obviously, if the Soviet press is shocked by the fact that school children are wearing crosses and that thousands of them are sold annually in Orenburg and intended largely for children,[30] then the religious issue can by no means be simply reduced to one involving just "grandmothers and grandfathers." The blame has to be laid at the door of the young or relatively young parents who cherish the wish to give their children a moral code grounded in religion. It is evident that the number of divorces caused by quarrels over religion has been increasing in the USSR. The organ of the Soviet trade unions reports the divorce of Mariya and Petr Lukyanenko, who could not get along with each other because she was a believer and he an atheist. Then there is Aleksander and Nina Shuplenov, who have five children, and Dimitri and Lyudmila Ryazan, who divorced on similar grounds. The same thing happened in the family of P. Klimenkov, with the only difference, however, that the quarrel did not lead to divorce, although the family was split into two camps.[31] "Father and mother started to fight over their daughter. Father used to read fascinating fairy tales to Tanya, but mother dinned into her head: 'Hail Mary, full of grace...' Father used to take the little girl to matinees, whereas mother dragged her by the hand to church."[32] This is the account of what had been happening in the household of the young doctor, M. E. Muranova, and her husband, a Party member and teacher of history. The conflict assumed such proportions that the couple divorced, and the father re-

---

[29] *Krasnaya zvezda*, February 14, 1965.
[30] *Izvestia*, November 28, 1965.
[31] *Sovetskiye profsoyuzy*, No. 8, 1963, pp. 16—17.
[32] *Pravda*, November 2, 1962.

ceived custody of his daughter. This shows that divorce on religious grounds is recognized in the Soviet Union.

The Soviet authorities are not only interested in cases in which a religious conflict has sprung up. They also interfere with the life of families in which both parents try to give their children a religious education. From its own atheist point of view the Soviet press is absolutely right in proposing, on the basis of Article 227 of the RSFSR Penal Code, to bring to court the case of a bricklayer named I. Shevchenko who brought up all six of his children in a strictly Orthodox spirit and let his daughter marry a young student at a seminary.[33] The inhabitants of the town of Buguruslan also wanted to bring an action in court against the Old-Believer, P. Samartsev, for bringing up his children according to religious precepts, and who refused to let them wear Young Pioneer ties. Yet, no matter what the future of these children is going to be, a spark of religion has been kindled in their souls.[34] In the village of Rudakovo in Gorky Oblast there lives the Zauzolkov family. The children never go to the cinema, do not join in the social life of the pupils, and read only religious books. The family is said to belong to an underground religious organization.[35]

Concerned over the large number of such families, the authorities have resorted to punishment by the arm of the law. Recalcitrant parents are brought to trial, and a most revealing case of this kind was that of forester Dimitri Sokhranyaev in Pskov Oblast, who brought up his children strictly according to the rules of the Orthodox Church, for which reason he was accused of "morally mutilating his children." The latter were taken away from their parents, who were still relatively young and had been brought up under the Soviet regime. The fact that Sokhranyaev had formerly been an activist and convinced atheist lent particular interest to the proceedings, and made his "crime" all the more heinous in the eyes of the press.[36]

Another development that is reported in Soviet newspapers is the appearance of illegal religious literature which young people help to distribute. It is said to be printed in the town of Maikop and to contain mainly religious excerpts from the Bible, and psalms. It is smuggled into the pockets and desks of pupils and teachers during classes.[37]

Against this background of religious activity it does not seem strange that during a lesson devoted to Russian culture in the eighteenth century, a young Soviet teacher should let his pupils read a text dealing with the self-educated inventor, Kulibin, who built a clock with a small door from which angels emerge when the clock strikes the hour, remove the stone from God's tomb and sing "Christ has risen." It is obvious that there are enough forces among the young

---

[33] *Nauka i religiya*, No. 5, 1963, p. 47.

[34] *Komsomolskaya pravda*, July 3, 1963.

[35] *Sovetskaya Rossiya*, September 27, 1962.

[36] *Selskaya zhizn*, June 14, 1962.

[37] *Uchitelskaya gazeta*, February 16, 1963.

generation to wage a relentless fight for a new triumph of the Orthodox Church in the USSR.[38]

As a final witness we may quote a correspondent of the Soviet army newspaper. What he says provides a clue to the present mood of young Soviet believers. The correspondent had a talk with a soldier who was a member of the Orthodox Church. The conversation lasted a long time and ended with the soldier saying to the major: "I am sorry for you, comrade major, you have learnt nothing in life."[39]

From the above it can be seen that those of the Soviet young generation who belong to the Orthodox Church are playing a decisive role in the country's spiritual renewal. There is some evidence too, that this is not a sporadic phenomenon but a widespread movement that has been going on under the surface of Soviet life. It is too early to say whether it is already an organized movement, but at any rate it is an irreversible process that will triumph in the end.

---

[38] *Ibid.*

[39] *Krasnaya zvezda*, February 14, 1965.

The Rejuvenation of the Russian Orthodox Clergy

Nadezhda Teodorovich

In recent years the ranks of the Russian Orthodox priesthood have been swelled by an increasing number of young people, some of them in their early twenties, and bishops who have been ordained at the age of thirty or no longer uncommon.

This phenomenon might be described as a revival of a tradition in the Russian Orthodox Church dating back long before the Revolution. Although in the past it was customary to appoint mainly elderly members of the clergy to bishoprics and other senior positions, some members of the ecclesiastical hierarchy were quite young. In the 17th century, Dmitri, Metropolitan of Rostov, was the prior of a monastery at the age of 25; in the 19th century, Tikhon Zadonsky was appointed a bishop when he was 37, and Filaret, the Metropolitan of Moscow, was consecrated at the age of 40. In the following century there was a Metropolitan of Kiev who had been the head of a seminary at 25 and was made a bishop at 40. Among the bishops who perished during the persecution of the church under Lenin and Stalin were twenty-one who were aged between 32 and 49 at the time of their consecration before the Revolution. According to information to be found in the directory of the Holy Synod for the year 1917, 84 per cent of this group of 74 bishops who lost their lives were under 49 years old when consecrated. Fourteen per cent were aged between 50 and 59, and 2 per cent beetween 60 and 70.

It is not surprising that many young people decided to enter the Church in pre-Revolutionary Russia: the entire culture which permeated the education system, the family and national way of life, tended to produce idealists strongly attracted to a life "not of this world." Very often, indeed, the priesthood was a hereditary tradition, and it must be remembered also that the church schools offered the chance of education and advancement to even the poorest sections of the population.

The upheaval of 1917 changed all this: the Church was stripped of her possessions and privileges, and anyone who served her was automatically charged with "counter-revolutionary activities."

Statistics on the average age of those who took holy orders during the period 1917 to 1940 are not readily available. There was, however, a fairly considerable influx of young blood into the hierarchy until the death of Patriarch Tikhon in 1925, and this helped to compensate for the earlier decimation of the clergy.

When the Moscow Patriarchate was formed in 1927 as the state-approved organ of ecclesiastical administration, the criterion of appointment to senior posts in the hierarchy was political reliability, i.e. the degree of subservience to the

35

interests of the Soviet regime. The bishops who composed the Provisional Patriarchal Synod at the time ranged in age between 50 and 65; otherwise no further information on the background or age of the ecclesiastical hierarchy becomes available until the outbreak of the Second World War, when the Church was allowed to become active once again, as a means of bolstering the national morale.

A complete list of the diocesan bishops in the Soviet Union was published for the first time by the Moscow Patriarchate in 1949, and the composition by age-group was given as follows:

30—49 years old..............	9 per cent
50—69 „ „	60 „ „
70—89 „ „	30 „ „
90—99 „ „	1 „ „

The majority were priests who had survived the years of persecution, while the youngest among them (up to 55 years old) were bishops who studied partly in the pre-Revolutionary theological schools and had entered the Church during the period of its greatest tribulations (1926—1930), former Uniate priests who were "reunited" with the Moscow Patriarchate in 1946, and those who took vows during the war or had been ordained outside the Soviet Union.

In the immediate post-war years, numerous new recruits joined the ranks of the Orthodox clergy, thanks to the special pastoral courses and the activity of the theological colleges which opened later, between 1945 and 1947. The products of this training programme were nearly all men in their thirties at least, many of whom had been connected with the Church or had even been priests before. Many had distinguished war records and had held responsible posts. It was from this group that the top posts in the Moscow Patriarchate were filled in the years following. Those who had been trained in the theological colleges and who graduated with distinction went on to theological academies, and the most talented were made bishops. The first bishops of this "new generation" included Mikhail Khub, who graduated from a theological academy at the age of 38, Aleksii (Konoplev) at the age of 44, and Fedosii (Pogorsky) at 47. The emergence of these men during the 1950's was the first sign of the "rejuvenation" of the episcopacy.

Nothing in the subsequent career of these younger members of the hierarchy justifies the charge that they were guilty of political self-seeking. Some, indeed, fell foul of the Soviet authorities. An abortive attempt was made to push Bishop Mikhail into the political arena in the course of his duties by appointing him to a foreign diocese, but he was abruptly recalled to the Soviet Union and shortly afterwards assigned menial diocesan duties which promised no privileges whatsoever. Indeed, the Soviet press conducted a smear campaign against Mikhail, accusing him of various offences, including moral turpitude. No such charges are ever brought against those bishops who serve the Soviet state well.

A new page in the history of the Church was opened on the death of Stalin in 1953. With Khrushchev's rise to power an attempt was made to win public support, including that of the religious believers. After Khrushchev signed the Party Central Committee decree of November 10, 1954, in which the attitude of the state towards religious activities was relaxed, a brief but effective "thaw" began for the Church. Persecution of believers was dropped and young people began to apply for admission to theological colleges in quite considerable numbers. In March 1961, the journal *Voprosy filosofii* (Questions of Philosophy) noted that until 1957 the number of applications for entry to theological colleges grew continuously, and while on a visit to England in 1956, Metropolitan Pitirim stated that those desiring to gain admittance to the college in his Belorussian diocese outnumbered the places available by three to one.

Some of the reasons impelling young people to take holy orders may be gleaned from the pages of the Soviet press: "I was blessed for nine years to serve God. I believe with all my heart in God and His Divine Power," declares one young man.[1] Another said, referring to the propagators of atheism: "They have me on edge. To tell the truth, I don't want people like that bragging later on how they did their job by re-educating us."[2] And a young worker named Bondarenko actually went to his local Komsomol committee to find out what the regulations were for entering a theological seminary. "And why did you make up your mind to go there?" they asked. "I'm told it's interesting," he answered.[3]

The general impression gained is that these youngsters are motivated by a belief in God, the inspiring idea of being on the side of the "underdog" and, possibly, the old Russian concept of "going to the people" and bringing them enlightenment, in this case, religious enlightenment. But most of all it is a protest against restraints on the individual's independence and right to choose his own way of life, together with a genuine interest in matters of theology. Whatever the reasons, there is no doubt that the Soviet leaders are perturbed by this appeal of religion to a section of the country's youth. It is a threat to the Party's attempt to indoctrinate the oncoming generation. This was the reason behind the official decision in 1958 to close down theological colleges, and the renewed attacks in the press on young believers.

The Episcopate of the Moscow Patriarchate

The steady increase in the number of younger bishops comprising the Patriarchate may be seen from the fact that whereas, according to a rough estimate, in 1949 only 9 per cent were aged between 30 and 49, in 1960 and 1965 this percentage had risen to 15 and 28 per cent respectively. Thirty per cent of the bishops were aged between 70 and 89 in 1949, 33 per cent in 1960 and 23 per cent in 1965. These figures suggest that there is a deliberate policy to gradually replace all the older members of the hierarchy by young men, and many bishops who have not

---

[1] *Komsomolskaya pravda*, December 4, 1959.

[2] *Nauka i religiya*, No. 8, 1963, p. 77.

[3] *Komsomolskaya zhizn*, No. 11, 1963, p. 10.

yet reached retirement age are being "put out to grass." The educational level of the "new blood" in the Patriarchate is markedly superior to that of the older members. During the period 1941–1952 only 36.5 per cent of members of the Patriarchate had studied theology at a university, compared with 44.1 per cent in 1965. Whereas those with no more than a theological education up to secondary level made up 32.7 per cent in 1941–1952, this percentage fell to 22.8 in 1953 and to 19.0 in 1965. In the case of those with a higher secular education the percentages for the same years were 11.5, 27.1 and 5.0 respectively. There was relatively little fluctuation in the case of those with a secondary secular education— 7.7 per cent in 1941–52 and 8 per cent in 1965. The higher educational level of the members of the Patriarchate in 1965 is very clearly indicated by the fact that 24.0 per cent of their number had both a secular and a theological higher education compared with only 11.5 per cent in the 1941–52 period and 17.1 per cent in 1953.

Some of the newly-appointed young bishops held posts in the state administration and worked in various specialist positions before entering the Church. The example of Bishop Leonid (Polyakov) is typical of this new, highly-educated type. He was formerly a doctor, graduated from a medical institute in 1939, and prior to this had studied chemistry at another university. While practising medicine he took an extramural course in theology and was ordained a bishop in 1959. The question naturally arises: what induced this man to give up a good profession for an ecclesiastical career not exempt from dangers? The administrative duties entrusted to him from the first—the office of Vicar of the Moscow diocese and Head of the Patriarchate Department for Administration would tend to suggest that Bishop Leonid was recruited into the ranks of those "bureaucrat" bishops who are the eyes and ears of Party surveillance. However, he did not remain in this job very long, but was soon transferred to Perm, where he is presently engaged on research into Church history, after having obtained a doctorate in this subject. Bishop Mikhail of Stavropol, mentioned above, also has a secular education in two separate fields. While he was "in the world" he studied in a university department of geology and mineralogy, after which he graduated from the Foreign Languages Institute. It is highly significant that both these bishops, and others who possess an advanced education and a higher theological training, occupy lowly diocesan posts in the Soviet Union. Apparently genuine scholarship and a true vocation for the priesthood are not compatible with the political "wheeling and dealing" in which some of their colleagues are engaged. The biographies of this latter type of bishop generally omit information about their educational background. There are also a number of young men aged not more than 37, such as Metropolitan Nikodim, Bishop Aleksii and others, who are among this group of bishops fulfilling political functions in the Moscow Patriarchate. At the same time it must be remembered that among the bishops belonging to the Patriarchate there is a also relatively large number of persons ordained as priests or monks at a young age who devoted their entire lives to the Church long before they became bishops. As far as may be estimated from study of the rather sparse data on the backgrounds of members of the episcopate, it appears that this latter category has composed about 53.3 per cent since 1953, as opposed to 28.4 per cent in the period 1941–1952.

At first sight the obviously growing tendency towards the "rejuvenation" of the episcopate in the Soviet Union might appear to be a wholly positive and promising development in the life of the Orthodox Church, analogous to the emergence of young bishops in the 18th and 19th centuries, and at the beginning of the 20th century, at a time when an influx of young men gave the Church a new aura of holiness and, later on, a band of martyrs. In these previous times the entry of devoted young men into the higher ranks of the clergy was a reflection of a revival in religious faith among the people. In the present instance, however, the careers of some of these young bishops in the Soviet Union today show that since the end of the Second World War many political figures have infiltrated the Patriarchate and are mainly to be found among the young generation. These young bishops are members of various political committees which often serve the international policy aims of the Soviet Government. The activities of these committees tend to distort the functions of the Church in the Soviet Union and thereby mislead the world public. This in turn causes believers in the USSR to turn to any available source, even at international level, in an effort to ascertain the truth about the actual state of the Church in their country. Those in the upper ranks of the clergy who are recognized to be genuine servants of the Church are respected, but those who are seen to be purely careerist bureaucrats are scorned, and dubbed "red cassocks". It is the ranks of the "red cassocks" that are being replenished by young bishops. This is a very important feature to bear in mind in any discussion of the "rejuvenation" of the clergy in the Soviet Union. It means that in this process the state tends to increase its influence over the Church, more particularly in the higher reaches of the hierarchy. At a lower level the picture is rather different.

The Theological Colleges

Since the 1950's the teaching staffs of the ecclesiastical schools in the Soviet Union have begun to be replenished by their own graduates. According to information given in the Soviet press, the Russian Orthodox Church has in recent years trained 370 candidates of theology, and 19 masters and 8 doctors of theology and ecclesiastical history.[4] In the 1950's Bishop Mikhail (born 1906) and, more recently, Pimen (born 1923) and others all taught in these theological colleges. The rector of the Moscow Theological Academy and Seminary is the young Bishop Filaret (born 1929), who completed his higher theological education in 1950. Only a trained theologian can judge whether the instructors at these colleges are adequately versed in their subject, but the fact remains that theologians from the Soviet Union make quite a good showing at international theological conferences and gatherings, which shows that the level of their scholarship is appreciable.[5] Quite young Soviet theologians are to attend the forthcoming Orthodox

[4] *Ibid.*, p. 11.

[5] For accounts of contacts between the Leningrad Theological Academy and Western theologians, see *Zhurnal Moskovskoy Patriarkhii*, October, 1958, p. 14, and October, 1960, p. 63.

ecumenical council, although it is hard to say to what extent they may have a political role to play at such an international gathering.

Laymen in the Soviet Union are also found on the staff of theological colleges. One such example is V. I. Talyzin, a graduate of the Moscow Electrical and Machine-Building Institute and the Institute of Mechanization and Electrification. Talyzin worked in various factories before deciding in 1946 to enter a theological academy from which he graduated in 1950 at the age of 46, becoming a lecturer in canon law and, later on, in theology. He became the victim of a number of attacks in the Soviet press for having "forsaken the task of Soviet construction for the teaching of obscurantism." As is common in such cases, he was accused in addition of being an alcoholic.

Archpriest Professor A. D. Ostapov (born 1930) might serve as an example of the young teachers of theology. After graduating he stayed on as a student teacher, became a lecturer at the age of 26, specializing in ancient church history and the New Testament. At 33 he was director of the extra-mural department of the Moscow Theological Academy and of its church archeological study centre.

Ostapov is just one of the numerous young people who will one day be highly-learned theologians. They, least of all among the Orthodox clergy, are likely to become in any way involved in politics, although there are among the theologians, as among the bishops, those who either sincerely or insincerely strive to demonstrate the compatibility between the Soviet system and the mission of the Church. A figure of this type was the recently deceased A. F. Shishkin (born 1897), a lecturer at the theological academy. In 1919 he graduated in history and philology, and after serving in the Red Army entered the Pedagogical Institute of Music to train as a conductor. After completing the course he began studying the Soviet Constitution at a theological academy, took a degree in theology and became a lecturer in the subject, also giving courses on the Constitution and becoming conductor of the Metropolitan Church Choir in Leningrad. He regularly delivered lectures at the theological academy on current affairs, Soviet foreign policy, and the achievements of the government at home. The fact that this versatile figure was entrusted with both a course on the Soviet constitution and lectures on political subjects indicates that he enjoyed the special trust of the Party authorities. Nor was he the only example of such a curious combination of functions, which was fairly common during the 1920's at the time of the reformist movement for "renewal" which sought a *modus vivendi* with the Soviet authorities.

This is not to suggest that the theological colleges in the Soviet Union fail to instil into their students a profound and conscious sense of religion, while at the same time equipping them with the knowledge necessary to them as members of Soviet society. The evidence that the colleges are doing their job may be found in the attacks levelled against them in the Soviet anti-religious press.[6]

---

[6] See *Molodoy kommunist*, No. 2, 1966.

The Rank and File Clergy

The *Zhurnal Moskovskoy Patriarkhii* (Journal of the Moscow Patriarchate) never publishes any reports on the work of the ordinary priests who after graduating from the theological seminaries go out to the parishes. Paradoxically enough, it is to the anti-religious articles in the Soviet press that we have to turn in order to discover something of their activities. For example, it was the journal *Komsomolskaya zhizn* which revealed in 1963 that during the preceding few years seminaries in the Soviet Union had graduated over 2,000 priests. The anti-religious articles in the press provide an idea of the type of person who works in the parishes throughout the country. A description is given of a certain young Father Ioann who came to the tiny village of Volchanka on the steppes bordering the Volga to take the place of the old priest there. He was just 25 years of age, well-built and with a striding gait. But he had a serene, tender look about him and a fine, deep voice. Father Ioann's refinement and education assured him the respect of the young faithful, and his impeccable knowledge of ritual put him on good terms with the strict, pettifogging old women. He became an unquestionable authority for everyone. Then there is the mention of another priest who at first startled his parishioners by his youth. However, his sermons, and especially his burning desire to deal a blow at the "propagators of atheism," won many over in his favour. The "propagators of atheism" were afraid of a clash and consequently stayed away from the village. This new breed of young, educated priests seems to be causing the Soviet authorities some concern. It is stated in the press that they deliver their sermons spontaneously, without notes, as Party speakers usually do, and know how to marshal their arguments effectively. The complaint is voiced that these priests have learnt the way to work with light entertainment media. Young pastors play songs on the concertina and use tape recorders on which they have recorded not only hymns but also contemporary music. They stage musical evenings and thus establish contact with their parishioners. They have a modern approach, are familiar with science and not overawed by the achievements of the cosmonauts. They can talk about football and often play themselves; they drive cars and are generally abreast of the times. Most important, they know how to organize a choir. A choir song always reaches the heart, and there are young people's choirs to be found in the Soviet Union which are directed by young priests.

For these reasons the Party ideologists and lecturers in atheistic propaganda are having to be more and more on their mettle. There is a highly interesting new play called, "Everything is Left to the People" by S. Aleshin, in which the author lets all the rejoinders by the young Father Serafim go unchallenged by his adversary in argument, the materialist academician, F. Dronov. The play was withdrawn on the order of the authorities and Aleshin was told to rewrite it. But the first version is convincing proof that the young priest in the Soviet Union is no longer just a figure of fun who commands no respect. He is recognized as a doughty opponent in the ideological polemic. Even an official Soviet journal like *Science and Religion* admits, when referring to young priests: "The young enthusiasts dream eagerly of how they are to be sent into the fastnesses of the provinces to bring the world of God to the people..."[7] The readiness of these "enthusiasts" to stand up for their religion and to defend the Church is illustrated by a conversation reported in the Soviet press between a certain A. Osipov, a former archpriest and inspector at a theological academy who subsequently left the Church. Osipov writes:

> During a visit to me on December 3, the day after I broke with the Church, three students on the second course at the Theological Academy stated first and foremost: "We understand that it is natural to leave the Academy if your views on religion have changed; but we cannot imagine how you could join with the atheists in their struggle against religion. The church is unevenly matched with atheism in this struggle. And a struggle with an adversary who is not given a fair chance is a dishonest contest. Are you really going to participate in a dishonest struggle?[8]

Such was the reaction to Osipov, who is probably the biggest of the fish whom the Soviet authorities have landed among the seventy-odd apostates who have recounted their reasons for leaving the Church in the pages of the press over the last few years. In most cases these renegade priests lacked the endurance to serve the Church in an atmosphere of hostility on the part of the authorities, but some were persons who had been selected by the authorities to enter seminaries and then, after being ordained, to "break with religion" ostentatiously and provide fuel for atheist propaganda. Of course, among the apostates are those who were looking for a "quite haven" and a secure existence in the bosom of the Church, and who, on finding that this was not to be, seek other, easier paths in life. Young people are among these deserters, but they feature too among those on the side of religion, many of them in jails and labour camps.[9]

The situation of the Church in the Soviet Union is complex. It cannot be stated in terms of black and white; there are many contradictory and confusing facets to be considered. In the midst of ever-expanding technology and estrangement of man from his inner self there is an urge on the part of many to try to wed age-old beliefs to new conditions and to forge new philosophical approaches. The longing for new moral standards, uncompromised by the corruption of the past, and the search for truth in all things is a phenomenon to be widely observed among the Soviet population, especially of the young generation. This effort to regenerate spiritual values is evident among many of the young priests who desire to revitalise their Church. The spirit of reform is affecting the preparations for the ecumenical council to be held by the Orthodox Church, and even among the priests of the Moscow Patriarchate itself there was recently some reflection of this spirit on a small scale: two priests of the Moscow diocese, N. Eshlimen and G. Yakunin, sent an "Open Letter" to the Patriarch of Moscow, Aleksii, and to all bishops of the Russian Orthodox Church, together with a "Declaration,"

---

[7] *Nauka i religiya*, No. 7, 1964, p. 76.

[8] *Izvestia*, December 20, 1969.

[9] See N. A. Teodorovič, "Processi e condanne contro sacerdoti e credenti nell' URSS," *Russia Cristiana*, Bergamo, Nos. 73—74, 1966.

submitted to the Chairman of the USSR Supreme Soviet, Podgorny, the Chairman of the USSR Council of Ministers, Kosygin, and the USSR Procurator-General, Rudenko. These two men were bold enough to "break the bonds of silence," as they themselves put it, in order to write that the church of the Moscow Patriarchate was "seriously and dangerously ill," and that this malady was imaged forth in the way the Patriarch and top-ranking clergy have to lean over backwards in their efforts to maintain relations with an atheist state, and that the latter, in the shape of the Council for Russian Orthodox Church Affairs, exceeds its administrative prerogatives. They further stated that both the Patriarch and his bishops were to blame, through their opportunist behaviour, for the deliberate undermining of the Church, resumed with vigour by the state in 1957.

These outspoken priests are not alone, and such men are the only hope of the Church if she is to be regenerated.

In conclusion the following points deserve emphasis:

1. Despite the extremely difficult conditions with which the Orthodox Church in the Soviet Union has had to contend for almost a half century, the fount of spiritual resistance in it has not run dry.

2. This resistance is concentrated not only among the older clergy and faithful but among the younger generation, which is something the militant atheists had not banked on. It is a blow to see young people deliberately choose service to the Church as their path in life, despite having grown up entirely during the Soviet period.

3. In the light of this, the pessimistic conclusions to be found in the book by Professor de Vries would appear to require some modification. Writing in 1950 de Vries referred to the acute crisis that the Church would face when the elderly, who make up the bulk of the church-goers, die out.[10] In fact, the signs are that religious fiath has not died out, but has been steeled by decades of persecution. The Orthodox clergy is managing to recruit new members among certain sections of Soviet youth. This new blood promises to be steadfast and equipped to meet the challenges of modern mass society, unlike the older generation, who are less able to find a *modus vivendi* between the Church and the world about them. This holds out the hope that the Orthodox Church will rise to a new level.

---

[10] Wilhelm de Vries, S. J., *Christentum in der Sowjetunion*, Heidelberg, 1950, p. 160.

Pseudo-Religious Rites Introduced by the Party Authorities

Nikita Struve

The Soviet press has often discussed ways and means of ousting religious rites by the introduction of a special "communist" marriage ceremony, and holidays designed to replace the traditional ones of the Church calendar. This has always been part of the anti-religious campaign aimed at weaning the population away from the Church. The communist authorities have had to recognise that it is not enough to oppose such rites as baptism and the marriage ceremony; something had to be found to fill the void, and this has led to the introduction of civil ceremonies that, so it is hoped, will help to cut off the young generation still further from the Church and age-old traditions that lend an element of colourfulness and romance to everyday life.

Civil ceremonies were experimented with as early as the 1920's and met with very little success. In their revolutionary ardour, the communists tried to do away with the christening ceremony and even with Christian names, and,, of course, some new civil holidays have become traditional in the Soviet Union since the Revolution. Before 1917 Russia was a theocratic state in which the religious and civil spheres were not separated. Church holidays were observed by all citizens, and even the celebrations, such as anniversaries etc., of the temporal power had a religious flavour and were accompanied by religious ceremonies.

The October Revolution put an end to this, and such national holidays as May Day and the Anniversary of the October Revolution itself were introduced, all completely devoid of any religious content. This is not peculiar to the Soviet Union; revolutions invariably bring similar innovations in their train. In France, for instance, the greatest national holiday is of revolutionary origin and has nothing to do with religion. At the same time, however, the 14th of July does not set out to rival any Church holiday. The population regards the state and the Church holidays as wholly separated but not mutually exclusive. The same attitude is found in the Soviet Union, where the population considers national and Church holidays as belonging to entirely different spheres. The following extract from the *Derevensky Dnevnik* (Country Diary) by the Soviet writer, Efim Dorosh, illustrates this well. The author describes the celebration of the Church holiday of the Transfiguration in a small village where there is a collective farm. Not one of the farm workers went out to the fields that day, and the author records his conversation with one of the peasant women:

> We had a talk about it with Natalya Kuzminichna; she told us: "I don't know really what holiday it is exactly; all I know is that it's an important one, and that it would be a sin to work". I said to her: "But you never go to church and goodness knows, it's probably ages since you've been to confession. What can this holiday

mean to you? Just wait till the October Anniversary comes round, and then you can celebrate." But she only laughed at me, and of course I could not make her change her attitude.[1]

This passage shows that the very idea of a national holiday replacing a religious ceremony does not even enter the head of an ordinary woman on a collective farm. She acknowledges that the things that are Caesar's must be rendered unto Caesar, but to God the things that are God's. And this strict separation of Church holidays from state ones in the minds of the people has made it clear to the anti-religious propagandists that it is absolutely essential to introduce new holidays and customs capable of supplanting religious rites. They want to establish communist traditions that can successfully rival the ancient ones. In the beginning, however, this decision caused dissent among the atheists, the majority of whom held that the invention of new rites would be tantamount to a return to religion in the shape of a surrogate for the latter. But these objections were overruled and after lively discussion in the press it was decided in 1964 to submit the plan for introduction of new holidays to the republican councils of ministers for approval. Now the USSR Supreme Soviet introduces a new national day of celebration almost every month. There is already "Woman's Day," "Miner's Day," "Fishermen's Day," "Railwaymen's Day," and "Militia Day," etc., and most sections of the working population are honoured in this way. According to a recent study, which contains a detailed survey of pseudo-religious rites in the Soviet Union, there are twenty-two of these "Days."[2]

However, this plethora of new-fangled celebration days is more a propaganda stunt than a budding tradition. Persons who have visited the Soviet Union in recent years report that the new holidays and civil rites play little or no part in everyday life. They do not appear to have taken root. There is a so-called "Palace of Happiness" in Leningrad, where the newly-invented civil marriage ceremony is performed in elaborate fashion, but there are not many of these palaces so far because they are expensive to put up. The *zvezdiny* rite (which is a revival of the *Oktyabriny* christening ceremony of the 1920's, with the only difference that babies are no longer given extraordinary, "revolutionary" names) is observed, for instance, in the Seredino-Budsky raion of Kharkov Oblast, but is said to be entirely unknown anywhere else round about.[3] This artificial process of imposing new customs does not evoke much enthusiasm among the population, as official sources admit. The conversion of the carnival season into a 'Russian Winter Festival' "has killed off this popular custom at the roots,"[4] and a folk-lore specialist writes that "our new holidays and rites are threatened by a danger that has already started to make itself apparent. We have in mind the possibility that they will become rather desiccated and conventional, and turn into tedious bureaucratic measures."[5] This waning of interest is demonstrated in a report from a

[1] *Literaturnaya Moskva*, 1956, p. 616.

[2] "Le nuove feste e i nuovi riti sovietici," *Russia Cristiana*, No. 67–68, Bergamo, 1965.

[3] *Izvestia*, December 20, 1964.

[4] D. Balashov, "The Traditional and the Modern," *Nauka i religiya*, No. 12, 1965, p. 30.

[5] *Sovetskaya etnografiya*, No. 6, 1963, p. 23.

correspondent in Grodno, who writes that the first few marriages were indeed performed with much pomp at the Grodno "Palace of Matrimony" but subsequently they became a pretty dull, routine affair. Elsewhere it is stated bluntly: "So far it is possible to name only one successful experiment in transplanting an old rite onto the soil of new social relations. That is the New Year Tree."[6]

Thus, there is recognition among the ideologists that efforts to introduce new customs usually meet with little success. "This gives us something to ponder on," says one expert in a survey of new rites.[7] Already the more intelligent among the propagandists seem to have come to the conclusion that artificially-concocted customs conceived by the bureaucracy are scarcely likely to flourish. For practically half a century the Soviet authorities have been attempting the well-nigh impossible by introducing new customs etc. to replace time-hallowed observances, and the extent of their failure to fill the void is reflected in the works of such contemporary Soviet authors as Yefim Dorosh, Vladimir Soloukhin, and A. I. Solzhenitsyn. There are Soviet specialists who are capable of analysing the situation objectively and realistically, as is shown by the following extract from the leading atheist propaganda journal:

A rite is the symbolic and aesthetic expression (and manifestation) of collective social relations, of the collective essence of man, and the bonds linking him not only with his contemporaries but also with his ancestors. A rite is the thread of time by holding on to which people form a nation. A rite is created as the expression of the spirit, traditions and way of life of a society.[8]

This definition met with the disapproval of the editorial board of *Nauka i religiya*, and for good reason, because in the light of such an interpretation the present Soviet policy of introducing new customs appears hopeless and purposeless. Unfortunately, those with such a realistic approach remain "voices in the wilderness" in Soviet ideological circles.

The sterility of the new customs stems in no small degree from the fact that efforts are being undertaken to enforce them on the populace. A factory worker in Sumy Oblast writes:

I would like to call to your attention that my wife, Kozyk, Varvara Petrovna, gave birth to a daughter on October 31, 1964, our third child, and that on November 18, I submitted the documents to the Seredino-Budsky *Zags*[9]—both the notification of the birth and our marriage certificate. But they have not as yet issued a birth certificate for our daughter. Instead I am told, "the baby has to undergo *zvezdiny*, after which your daughter will be presented with a baby carriage and other gifts, in addition to the birth certificate. I categorically refused to have my daughter christened under such compulsion. At the *Zags*, however, they declared: "You will not get the birth certificate until you have the *zvezdiny* performed." And who thought up these *zvezdiny*, anyway?[10]

---

[6] D. Balashov, *op. cit.*, p. 29.

[7] *Sovetskaya etnografiya*, No. 6, 1963, p. 23.

[8] D. Balashov, *op. cit.*, p. 28.

[9] Registry Office of Births, Marriages and Deaths.

[10] *Izvestia*, December 20, 1964.

This case is the most striking example of objections to new, pseudo-religious rites. A rite without traditions, not grounded in history but imposed from above soon becomes a planned state "measure." Plans have to be fulfilled, and so coercion, softened by bribery, as in the case of the gifts at the *zvezdiny* ceremony, is resorted to. It goes without saying that such methods arouse suspicion towards the new rites, which seem to have sprung from nowhere. The whole problem represents a vicious circle from which the innovators can find no escape. To be sure, there are some Soviet social workers who realise the senselessness of artificially-created ceremonies. But what is the answer? To do without holidays or rites is impossible; life has to be made more colourful, especially as the time of noble sacrifice and heroic revolutionary deeds is over. One expert[11] has conceded that "nothing will come of inventing a marriage ceremony or any other custom," and suggests that the old, traditional ones be retained in a form suitable to Soviet society. This idea is less absurd than invention of totally new pseudo-religious rites, but is hardly likely to meet with much more success. According to this concept, a rite is only an incidental part of religious belief and is completely detachable from its original context. Its author may to some extent be right, but he nevertheless sees that traditional ceremonies such as christening and nuptial rites are indissolubly linked with Christianity. For this reason he does not propose that observances of Christian origin be adapted to communist requirements. Instead he clings to those observances that date back to pagan times. Why heathenism—itself a primitive form of religion—should be considered more suitable for a communist society than the Christian faith is not clear. Perhaps because paganism is long since dead and therefore no longer dangerous to Soviet ideology. Yet the Russian carnival survived into modern times not because it stood for the worship of the sun, as symbolized by the *blin* (pancake), but because it preceded Lent and was a psychologically necessary season of fun before parting with all the good things of this world during the ascetic period of the Church year. We have seen how transformation of the carnival into a "Russian Winter Festival" has failed in the Soviet Union. Balashov proposes that the old Slavonic *maslenitsa* period of revelry and pancake-making be converted into a modern observance lending some colour to Soviet life. But he has no suggestion as to how this is to be done. If *maslenitsa* is divorced from Lent, then it is likely to die out or survive merely as a seasonal culinary occasion that will be in time forgotten. He points, it is true, to the successful experiment in "transplanting an old custom onto the soil of new social relations" in the shape of the New Year Tree festival. But the Christmas or New Year tree is not such an old custom, nor is it specifically religious, and in Western countries it can easily be separated from the Church festival. Is it not possible, however, that the tree custom has become a Soviet tradition precisely because it is at least closely associated with the great Christmas festival and carries reminders of the latter? At any rate it is the only one that the Soviet regime has managed to introduce permanently.

The failure of the recent moves to conjure up new ceremonies devoid of all religious content for the Soviet citizen is bound up with the very meaning of a

[11] D. Balashov, *op. cit.*, p. 29.

rite. Balashov has been quoted above as referring to a "thread of time" by which nations are formed. This is true. A ceremonial observance links man to his fellows and to his ancestors; at Easter, for instance, Christians feel much closer to one another. They also feel close to those who are no longer with them, with those who once used to celebrate this festival. A religious rite is a thread that unwinds into the present from the depths of time. The Christian religious services can be traced back to the Jewish cult and beyond that all the way back to the ancient blood sacrifice to God. In the course of their historical evolution, Christian rites have accreted Greek culture and the individual stamp of each different country. And they are something else, too, which Balashov does not mention—a link with God. A rite unites mankind with a higher principle and a people senses this, even if it happens to forget the immediate meaning of some observance. In the Soviet Union Church rites survive not just because they are traditional or for aesthetic reasons. They exist primarily because they are felt, either vividly or vaguely, to be the visible, tangible expression of the higher meaning of life. If most Soviet parents have their babies baptised in church, it is because they desire consciously or unconsciously to impart some meaning to human life.

Faith, rites and culture are links in the chain leading to unison with God. Without faith there is no rite; culture fades away, and the resulting void is filled with chaos and moral decay. If a rite is torn from this chain it becomes no more than a museum exhibit, and this is the quandary of the Soviet propagandists and ideologists.

Changes in Soviet Medical Ethics
as an Example of Efforts to Find Stable Moral Values

Heinrich Schulz

This paper is based partly on material taken from the author's article "Medical Ethics in the USSR," which has appeared in the *Bulletin*, Vol. XII, No. 3, 1965, and *Review of Soviet Medical Sciences*, Vol. I, No. 3, 1964, published by the Institute for the Study of the USSR.

The origins of medical ethics lie far back in antiquity, when both healing and the professional ethics of the physician were associated with religion. It was Hippocrates who first laid down the main principles of medical ethics in his famous Oath almost five centuries before the birth of Christ (Cf. Appendix I). The link between medicine and religion in those days was close, as may be seen from Hippocrates' declaration, "The art of healing leads to piety and to a love of one's fellow men."[1]

The link between medicine and religion was maintained by the Christian Church: for centuries large numbers of physicians and apothecaries began their careers within monastery walls, and even when the training of medical students subsequently passed entirely into the hands of the universities, the influence of religion and the Church on the schooling of doctors and on their professional ethics remained. In the medical faculties of most universities in the West and pre-Revolutionary Russia, theology was taught in addition to medical subjects in order to instil Christian morals into aspiring doctors.

Later, following the example of the West, universities in the Russian Empire began to introduce so-called "faculty vows," based on the Hippocratic Oath, which young doctors were required to sign when receiving their medical diplomas, and in which they promised to observe medical ethics in the practice of their profession (Cf. Appendix II).

During the latter half of the nineteenth century the doctrine of materialism brought about a sharp change in the general attitude toward ethics. Whereas Kant considered ethics to be a "categorical imperative," a kind of compulsive force looming over mankind, according to the Marxist view ethics were merely rules of conduct which had no absolute validity but were dictated by class interest and class consciousness, and were dependent upon the economic, class, and political circumstances obtaining at a given period within a given nation or social group. For this reason, many doctors in the West and in the Russian Empire began to regard the ethics of their profession as outmoded and incompatible with the progress of medical science.

---

[1] Albert Moll, *Ärztliche Ethik*, Stuttgart, 1902, p. 397.

In 1917, after the October Revolution, the Soviet authorities abolished the "faculty vow" and dissolved the bond between religion and ethics. At first, courses in theology were superseded by so-called "rudiments of political knowledge" (*politgramota*), then replaced in turn by the study of dialectical and historical materialism. The professed aim of this measure was to facilitate the formation of a new, communist world outlook among young medical students. In addition, an intensive propaganda campaign was launched against religion and medical ethics. The Soviet press was the main vehicle of these attacks, but they were reinforced with meetings, lectures and open discussions, all designed to convince the medical community that the only ethics physicians could practice were communist ethics. N. A. Semashko, the founder of the Soviet health service, held that "the ethics of the Soviet doctor are the ethics of his socialist motherland, the ethics of the builder of the communist society; they are communist morals."[2] The Soviet experts on public health, Z. P. Solovev[3] and M. I. Barsukov,[4] held the same views. This Marxist-Leninist treatment of medical ethics amounted to a complete rejection of the advances made in medical ethics since the time of Hippocrates.

During the first decade of Soviet rule in Russia, most physicians who had been educated before the Bolsheviks seized power naturally resisted efforts by the People's Commissariat of Public Health to foist the communist version of medical ethics upon them. A leading exponent of this opposition was the well-known physician and author, V. V. Veresaev. Many writers and journalists then entered the dispute, one of the most notable being Boris Pilnyak, whose book, *Povest o nepogashennoy lune* (A Tale about an Unextinguished Moon) became widely known in 1926 for its treatment of medical ethics and the attitude adopted by the Soviet authorities on this issue. The open discussion on medical ethics lasted until the 1930's, and was particularly heated over the issue of medical secrecy.

Veresaev states that his individualism drew much criticism from Soviet health officials immediately following the revolution, both in private conversations and public debates.[5] These officials insisted that the government was only interested in the well-being of the collective, and Semashko, then People's Commissar for Health, called for the total abolition of medical secrets. Professor A. I. Abrikosov "expressed on behalf of the professors of Moscow complete solidarity with the People's Commissar, thereby considering the matter to all intents and purposes closed."[6] Veresaev, however, believed that when there is no threat of social harm, then the doctor is bound to keep any secret entrusted to him by the patient. "In practice, the point of view being energetically put forward by N. A. Semashko,"

---

[2] N. A. Semashko, *Izbranniye proizvedeniya* (Selected Works), Moscow, 1954, p. 130.

[3] Z. P. Solovev, *Voprosy zdravookhraneniya*, (Questions of Public Health), Moscow, 1940, pp. 118–121.

[4] M. I. Barsukov, *Velikaya Oktyabrskaya Sotsialisticheskaya Revolyutsiya i organizatsiya sovetskogo zdravookhraneniya* (The Great October Socialist Revolution and the Organization of Soviet Public Health), Moscow, 1951, p. 8.

[5] V. V. Veresaev, *Polnoye sobraniye sochinenii* (Complete Works), 3rd ed., Vol. II, Moscow, 1929, p. 5.

[6] *Ibid.*

wrote Veresaev, "is leading among the rank-and-file doctors to shocking irresponsibility and outrageous neglect of the entirely legitimate rights of the patient."[7]

During the initial years of Soviet rule in Russia and until the 1930's, there was also frequent debate of the question of medical morality. Kharkov professor V. Ya. Danilevsky's book, *Vrach, ego prizvaniye i obrazovaniye* (The Physician, His Calling and Education), was published in 1921; in 1925 and 1930 a series of articles appeared in Leningrad entitled *Vrachebnaya taina i vrachebnaya etika* (Medical Secrecy and Medical Ethics), and books entitled *Meditsinskiye rabotniki; sotsialno-gigienicheskiye i klinicheskiye ocherki* (Medical Workers; Socio-Hygienic and Clinical Essays), *Trud i byt sovetskogo vracha* (The Work and Life of the Soviet Doctor), and others were published in Kharkov. S. S. Utkin, a contemporary Soviet expert on professional ethics, has criticized these publications on methodological grounds,[8] charging Danilevsky, for example, with "narrow-minded scholasticism," "neo-positivism," "indifference to politics," and unfamiliarity with dialectical and historical materialism." Utkin took particular exception to Danilevsky's assertion that neither materialism nor any other speculative philosophical system should form an integral part of a physician's views,[9] and he condemned V. P. Osipov, a professor at the Leningrad Military Medical Academy, for stating in the preface to one work that if the question of medical secrecy is excluded from medical ethics, almost nothing of these ethics would remain, since everything else depends on the personal integrity and decency of the individual physician.[10]

According to Utkin, another Leningrad professor, G. I. Dembo, maintained that there can be no special ethics for a doctor other than humanitarian ethics, and that sooner or later professional medical ethics must disappear.[11] When speaking about "special ethics" Dembo apparently had in mind communist ethics, which in the 1920's those heading the Soviet public health system had tried to substitute for humanitarian morals.

The official Soviet stand during the 1920's on medical ethics was set forth in publications such as the first edition of the official encyclopedia, then edited by Semashko, in which it was stated that "according to the spirit of Soviet legislation, it is fundamentally impermissible to base professional obligations on the interests of the individual without regard for the general interest of the state."[12] It is further stated that "the Soviet doctor or medical worker has no right to invoke medical secrecy if a court or the investigating authorities demand certain information on a patient from him, or if an inquiry is made by administrative personnel or institutions (health departments)."[13] Finally, it is unequivocally declared

---

[7] *Ibid.*

[8] See S. Utkin, *Moralny kodeks i professionalnaya spetsifika morali* (The Moral Code and the Specific Nature of Professional Morals), Rostov, 1964.

[9] *Ibid.*, p. 7.

[10] *Ibid.*, p. 72.

[11] *Ibid.*, p. 73.

[12] *Bolshaya meditsinskaya entsiklopediya* (The Large Medical Encyclopedia), 1st ed., Vol. V, Moscow 1928, p. 681.

[13] *Ibid.*, p. 680.

that "the only approach toward the question of medical ethics that we can embrace is based on the needs of the state, founded on the class interests of the masses of the people."[14]

In accordance with this attitude, a decree of December 1, 1924, imposed a number of restrictions on the duty of the doctor to keep his vow of secrecy,[15] and during the period of so-called "class medicine" in the Soviet Union in the 1920's, Semashko, the People's Commissar for Health, was constantly rebuking doctors for their "levelling" (*uravnitelny*) approach to patients and their failure to distinguish between "kulaks," "middle peasants," and "poor peasants" (the different social groups of peasants before the collectivization of Soviet agriculture). He expressed deep regret that epidemics made it necessary to keep hostile class elements in hospitals, and insisted categorically on preferential medical treatment for workers and poor peasants.[16] Similarly, the first edition of the *Large Medical Encyclopedia* countenanced the practice of carrying out scientific experiments on both sick and healthy persons, merely commenting that "here the interests of the patients and the collective may collide, and the doctor is faced with the need to reconcile them as painlessly as possible."[17]

During the 1920's the policy of the Soviet public health authorities generally tended to reduce medical ethics to the level of relationships between the physician and the state. Medical ethics in the Soviet Union, according to Semashko, require the doctor to fulfil the "sacred duty" of defending the fatherland, and further the prophylactic trend in medicine, etc. The first edition of the *Large Medical Encyclopedia* gives as examples of unethical behaviour on the part of the doctor toward the state and society: refusal by city doctors to go and work in the country; use of state health institutions for treating private patients; issue of medical certificates to private patients enabling them to avoid military service or heavy work, etc.[18]

From the 1930's, and particularly during Stalin's reign of terror, medical ethics in the Soviet Union practically ceased to exist. Open discussions on the subject were banned, and political talks were held at medical institutions in their stead. It was shown in these talks that "class" medical ethics had outlived their usefulness and must be replaced by naturally humane "communist" morality. The flood of literature at that time which dealt with problems of medical ethics took pains to build up a model type of Soviet physician—the "Stakhanovite doctor,"[19] who was supposed to be a paragon of efficiency, "effectively using every minute of the working day, raising the norms for treating patients, mastering the techniques of his profession, combatting idleness, engaging in both criticism and self-criticism," etc. Ye. A. Barshteyn, author of a pamphlet about this new man, wrote that in order to be a "Stakhanovite doctor" one must above

---

[14] *Ibid.*, p. 682.

[15] *Ibid.*, pp. 682–683.

[16] N. A. Semashko, *op. cit.*, pp. 141–146, 166.

[17] *Bolshaya meditsinskaya entsiklopediya*, Vol. V, 1928, p. 685.

[18] *Ibid.*, p. 686.

[19] See Ye. A. Barshteyn, *Kakim dolzhen byt vrach stakhanovets?* (What Should a Stakhanovite Doctor Be Like?), Uralsk, 1936.

all "get rid of the remnants of notorious 'medical ethics' once and for all."[20] This official scorn for medical ethics and insistence that they be subordinated to the morality of the communist state led in the 1930's and during the postwar years to vicious persecution of many Soviet doctors. It is sufficient to recall how the Soviet medical press vilified Professors Levin and Pletnev and other doctors who had been found guilty at political trials in 1938, and Stalin's Kremlin doctors in 1953 who, though entirely innocent, were arraigned on trumped-up charges for purely political reasons. The Soviet medical press at that time was full of articles by Soviet doctors demanding severe punishment for their colleagues. In 1950, moreover, the press began fiercely denouncing such prominent physiologists as L. A. Orbeli, I. S. Beritashvili and P. K. Anokhin in the interests of the political line then being followed by the state.

Utkin points out that "notwithstanding the fact that during the period of the personality cult, works on the actual professional nature of medical morality were very seldom published, practical medical workers piously preserved the best ethical traditions, enriched them with the experience of the Soviet period, and developed new moral standards."[21] In this instance he has in mind primarily a book written by the prominent Soviet surgeon and oncologist, Professor N. N. Petrov, entitled *Voprosy khirurgicheskoy deontologii* (Questions of Surgical Deontology), the first edition of which appeared in 1944. This book is important as an attempt to partly rehabilitate medical ethics by defining the doctor-patient relationship anew. By "deontology" Petrov meant the principles of conduct for medical personnel aimed at maximum effectiveness of treatment, avoiding causing a patient mental suffering, eliminating errors in diagnosis, treating each patient as an individual, constantly striving to improve medical qualifications, etc.

A year later, in 1945, Semashko wrote an article entitled "On the Image of the Soviet Doctor," in which he expressed the view that "the duty of a doctor is religiously to keep any secret confided to him by a patient," although he made the reservation that "one thing is indisputable when deciding the question of keeping a medical secret: the interests of the collective are higher than the interests of the individual."[22] Even with this reservation, however, Semashko's revised opinion does not differ substantially from that expounded by Veresaev in the 1920's.

In 1945 Semashko also made an about-face in his views on "class medicine," maintaining that medical ethics should be above class contradictions,[23] and thereby even he, the founder of the Soviet health service and a prominent Party official, became more liberal in his attitude toward medical ethics. Semashko divided the principles of medical ethics into those concerning relations (a) between doctor and patient; (b) between the doctor and society, and (c) among doctors themselves. He considered the most important principles under the first heading to be that doctors and medical personnel should show concern for a patient's peace of

---

[20] *Ibid.*
[21] S. Utkin, *op. cit.*, p. 74.
[22] N. A. Semashko, *op. cit.*, p. 246.
[23] *Ibid.*, p. 130.

mind, give immediate medical aid to the sick and the wounded, be professionally competent, and perform their duties carefully and conscientiously. As may be seen from the above, Semashko wholeheartedly adopted Petrov's viewpoint, which illustrates anew the positive influence that may be exerted on the views of a Party official by a specialist.

This problem of the doctor-patient relationship in the Soviet Union has, in fact, been under discussion since the foundation of the Soviet state. Official propaganda in the medical press has always asserted that the Soviet Union is the only country where a correct doctor-patient relationship can be guaranteed, because "in a socialist society, economic, social, political, ideological, and racial barriers between doctors and the public disappear; relations between doctor and patient are not founded on the principle of buying and selling services, since the doctor is materially remunerated for his labours by the state."[24] Although this statement sounds all very well in theory, it is a fact that in practice a doctor who is turned into a state official frequently adopts a bureaucratic attitude toward his patients and loses interest in his work. Indeed, for many years now *Meditsinskaya gazeta* has been recording cases of "callous," "heartless," and "bureaucratic" treatment of patients by their doctors, and of unsatisfactory medical care in general. Citing many examples, Utkin notes that

> some Soviet doctors fail to observe the elementary rules of politeness, tact and humane treatment, and forget about the specific character of their noble profession. Although in general these doctors are frequently good workers, they nonetheless manage to distress both patients and colleagues by their roughness and lack of tact.[25]

He goes on to say that "one encounters instances of an unfeeling bureaucratic attitude on the part of doctors toward their patients, toward their requests and legitimate demands."[26] These examples serve to demonstrate that the maxim "good doctors under socialism, bad doctors under capitalism" is simply untenable, since an important role in the doctor-patient relationship is played by the personality and character of the physician himself.

In an article on medical ethics, written in 1962, a young Soviet doctor named Vitali Korotich recalls the scholar F. G. Yanovsky, who died in Kiev in 1928, and who in pre-revolutionary Russia had a reputation for being a man who was indifferent to money, very humane as a physician, and a genuinely kind person. By way of contrast Korotich also describes the head of a large Soviet medical school who always refused medical aid to patients unable to afford treatment.[27]

With regard to the second set of principles governing medical ethics (relations between the doctor and society), Semashko and others hold that "special relations are established between the doctor, the state, and society under socialism. Unlike a capitalist society, under socialism there is no antagonism between the interests

---

[24] *Bolshaya meditsinskaya entsiklopediya*, 2nd ed., Vol. XXXV, Moscow, 1964, p. 835.

[25] Utkin, *op. cit.*, p. 102.

[26] *Ibid.*, p. 103.

[27] *Yunost*, October, 1962.

of the physician (and the medical worker in general) and the state."[28] This conclusion has been reached on the strength of a statement contained in the *Programme of the Communist Party of the Soviet Union* : "The state takes it upon itself to look after the preservation and constant improvement of the people's health." Thus, according to Semashko and other theorists, in the Soviet Union the interests of the physician, society and the state coincide. In their view this obliges the Soviet doctor to take an active part in all administrative and social endeavours for maintaining the people's health. Therefore the Soviet doctor cannot keep secrets from the state. He is duty-bound to work for a healthier external environment, advancement of prophylaxis, and better working and living conditions. The Soviet doctor is thus bound to cooperate actively with government, Party, Komsomol and professional organizations in measures aimed at safeguarding the health of the population. These propositions clearly indicate that in the Soviet Union medical ethics are based on the principle that the doctor is not so much a member of the medical profession as a state official.

The third set of ethical principles is also dominated by state interests. Semashko and other Soviet medical writers maintain that in the Soviet Union doctors have no grounds for being on other than good terms with one other because private practice has been virtually abolished, thus doing away with professional competition motivated by greed. V. Grazhul, in an article for the second edition of the *Large Medical Encyclopedia*, wrote: "Tact, solidarity, a considerate attitude toward the rights and the reputation of a colleague—these are the kind of mutual relations between medical workers that conform to the standards of socialist communal life."[29] He continues:

> However, friendly relations between professional colleagues are incompatible with a spirit of conciliatoriness toward errors, not to mention concealment of the professional crimes of this or that medical worker. A doctor has no right to conceal, out of a false sense of loyalty to his colleagues, criminal acts by other medical workers or facts testifying to a careless attitude toward patients and neglect in the execution of their professional duties on the part of medical workers.[30]

Theoretically, of course, the abolition of private practice should help to reduce rivalry among doctors, although it must not be forgotten that in many cases the absence of competition has the negative effect of causing a person to lose interest in his work. Turning a doctor into a state official does not, however, prevent him from intriguing against his colleagues in order to improve his position or to move higher up on the professional ladder. In the Soviet Union such intrigues are fostered in large measure by the official practice of encouraging doctors—and other workers for that matter—to report on the professional shortcomings of their colleagues. A typical incident of this practice was related in the press in January 1966.[31] P. P. Kovalenko, a young Party lecturer in the faculty of hospital

---

[28] *Bolshaya meditsinskaya entsiklopediya*, 2nd ed., Vol. XXXV, Moscow, 1964, p. 837.
[29] *Ibid.*, p. 386.
[30] *Ibid.*, p. 387.
[31] *Izvestia*, January 15, 1966.

surgery at the Rostov Medical Institute, who wished to become head of this faculty and secure access to the scientific material amassed by his distinguished teacher, Professor Z. I. Katrashev, organized and led a slander campaign against the latter. As a result, Professor Katrashev was subsequently removed from his post. The nerve-racking experience caused him to die of a heart attack soon afterwards, and the slanderer, Kovalenko, got the job he was fighting for. He even went as far as to plagiarise the material gathered by his deceased rival in a book which he submitted in the hope of gaining a Lenin Prize.

The attentive reader of the Soviet medical press will find many similar cases. It is sufficient to recall that Lidiya Timashuk, herself a doctor, was awarded the Order of Lenin in 1953 for her part in bringing to light the alleged misdeeds of the Kremlin doctors.[32] That "state interests" may be in conflict with the accepted concepts of human ethics is readily apparent in the political trials, referred to above, which were organized against physicians in the Soviet Union.

In Utkin's book, mentioned earlier, there are a number of references to doctors "with a diploma and Party card in their pocket" heading medical institutions and permitting themselves "an uncalled-for, offensive tone in their dealings with medical personnel."[33] Such doctors demand subservience, and treat their subordinates condescendingly. *Meditsinskaya gazeta* also frequently records similar cases, and this shows that in state-run institutions, where private practice has been virtually abolished, it is possible for medical workers to be on less than good terms with one another. Referring to private practice, Utkin writes:

> One of the most harmful survivals of the past in the minds of some doctors is their attempt to use their humane speciality for private gain. They build their personal success on the grief and sufferings of others brought on by sickness. We have still not completely rooted out private practice. Some houses in large cities still bear signs offering medical treatment, and, of course, not free, but for commensurate material remuneration.[34]

Utkin blames the existence of private medical practice in the Soviet Union on "simpletons," who "rise to the bait" of private practitioners, and on some doctors who cling to a private-property attitude and morality. "They do not appreciate," he writes, "that they are causing great harm to the Soviet public health service and undermining its authority by supporting the senseless view that a family physician is more gentle and attentive to his patients than one who sees his patients at a polyclinic or hospital."[35] He goes on to advocate that private medical practice be abolished once and for all, on the ground that it is amoral. In this Utkin is backed by *Meditsinskaya gazeta*, which for a decade has been waging a determined, albeit unsuccessful, struggle against doctors in private practices.

---

[32] *Meditsinsky rabotnik* (now *Meditsinskaya gazeta*), January 13, February 24, 1953.

[33] S. Utkin, *op. cit.*, p. 102.

[34] *Ibid.*, p. 100.

[35] *Ibid.*

During the "thaw" following the death of Stalin, Soviet doctors, tired of lies, injustice, and hypocrisy, once again began to express their feelings about medical ethics on the pages of the medical press and in literary magazines, at congresses and at conferences. Their desire to revert to traditional medical ethics caused them to seek for universally valid standards of morality, and the young members of the profession were in the forefront of this movement. Vitali Korotich, whom we have quoted above, wrote, as a representative of these young people: "We studied at an excellent time. I first came to the institute in September 1953. Only a short time before, the most eminent Soviet physicians were being slandered...to such an extent that it was shameful for medicine. We had the good fortune to qualify as doctors during a period when eternal words and concepts were being purged of grime."[36] By "eternal words" Korotich apparently means the words from the Hippocratic Oath, which was the essence of the pre-Revolutionary faculty vows. He is not seeking any new definition for ethical concepts; it is clear to him that a doctor is "a complex not only of professional but also of moral qualities."[37] "I know of no other profession," he writes, "where questions of morals and professional skill are so closely interwoven."[38] His definition of a doctor's moral code is summed up in the words "unselfishness," "self-sacrifice," "devotion to duty," and "charity." Korotich is so concerned with problems of medical ethics that in addition to discussing them in the newspaper he also talks about them on Soviet television. Utkin points out that Soviet students are currently displaying a heightened interest in questions of professional ethics,[39] and he also relates how Soviet medical personnel have tried to form their own moral rules of conduct, similar to the former faculty vows.[40] An example of one such set of moral "commandments," drawn up by doctors at the Darnitsky Hospital in Kiev, was published in the December 18, 1962 issue of *Meditsinskaya gazeta* (Cf. Appendix III). These twelve commandments have much in common with the faculty vows, although worded differently. It is interesting to note, however, that they avoid touching on the question of medical secrecy. On the other hand, they are not steeped in official jargon, the usually omnipresent words "Soviet," "socialist," and "communist" being absent. The only phrase that has a Soviet flavour about it is "the present and the future belong to preventive medicine." Even this, however, was originally coined by the eminent Russian physician of the last century, N. I. Pirogov.

This quest after ethics by doctors and those in other professional groups in the Soviet Union (which has its counterpart in the wider search by the young for new religious and moral values) has caused the authorities to publish the so-called "moral code of builders of communism" (Cf. Appendix IV), which is described by *Izvestia* as containing "the basic human and moral standards evolved

---

[36] *Yunost*, October, 1962, p. 102.

[37] *Ibid.*, p. 100.

[38] *Ibid.*

[39] S. Utkin, *op. cit.*, p. 97.

[40] *Ibid.*, pp. 96, 97.

by the common people over thousands of years."[41] Nine out of the twelve points in the code do conform to this definition: they are acceptable both from the standpoint of humanitarian and religious morality. Only three points (1, 11 and 12) are purely communist in inspiration. It is the hope of the Party leaders that this code will deflect the various professional groups, especially young people, from the search for new moral and religious values. It is supposed to supersede the traditional religious moral code and to aid the Soviet authorities in imposing their own, communist set of values. Utkin professes that under Soviet conditions there is no need to equip the medical profession with special ethical norms such as those contained in the faculty vows, "because the foundation of their highly ethical conduct is the moral code of the builders of communism, and strict, conscious, and voluntary observance of its requirements."[42] He declares:

> The basis of the professional morals of the Soviet physician is his acute awareness of responsibility to the people, whom he is obligated to serve faithfully and truthfully, to the people who are building the most humane and just social order on earth—communism.[43]

Grazhul develops these ideas further and concludes that the main features of medical ethics in a socialist society

> "coincide with the moral code of the builders of communism, in which are contained such moral principles as devotion to the communist cause, conscientious work for the good of society, a profound sense of public duty, collectivism, comradely help, humanitarian relations between people, mutual respect, moral cleanliness, simplicity and modesty in one's personal and public life, etc."[44]

Grazhul goes on to say that "the outlook of the Soviet doctor is based on the doctrine of Marxism-Leninism and the achievements of the natural sciences: chemistry, physics, biology, and medicine. It develops during the course of a relentless struggle against such reactionary bourgeois theories as Malthusianism, vitalism and positivism."[45] Finally, he reminds us that the Soviet doctor "is not only a representative of a certain profession but above all a citizen of a socialist society."[46]

Besides these propaganda statements defining the ethics of the Soviet doctor, present-day Soviet public health theoreticians agree that

> "the Soviet doctor, having devoted himself to the preservation of the people's health, must be prepared at all times to render aid to the sick, increase his medical knowledge and raise his qualifications, refrain from using his knowledge to the detriment of society, to be a humanist and collectivist. He is required to understand

---

[41] *Izvestia*, July 30, 1961.
[42] S. Utkin, *op. cit.*, p. 97.
[43] *Ibid.*, p. 98.
[44] *Bolshaya meditsinskaya entsiklopedia*, 2nd ed., Vol. XXXV, Moscow, 1964, p. 835.
[45] *Ibid.*, p. 836.
[46] *Ibid.*, p. 835.

professional secrecy correctly, to be uncompromising with all that is antiquated and outmoded in medicine, and to seek new ways and means for ridding people of their ailments and diseases."[47]

This part of Soviet medical ethics, as we see, only amounts to a rephrasing of the Hippocratic Oath and the faculty vows. Indeed, as Grazhul points out, many Soviet institutions revived the tradition of faculty vows in 1964 "to accord with the principles of socialist medical ethics."[48]

To sum up: three distinct periods may be distinguished in the development of medical ethics in the Soviet Union during the last half-century:

1. 1917–1930: the Soviet government flatly denied the need for the existence of medical ethics, while the medical profession pressed for their complete retention;

2. 1931–1953: the Soviet government literally drove medical ethics underground; the medical profession tried to retain at least part of them by giving them different names ("deontology," "the outlook of the Soviet doctor," etc.);

3. 1954 to date: the medical community is engaged in a search for new professional standards, and the Soviet authorities are trying to adjust themselves to the situation.

It would seem that the above course of events has now almost come full circle with a reversion to many of the traditional ethical standards. Medical secrecy, totally rejected shortly after the Revolution, is now recognized, albeit with a number of reservations, as the "sacred duty" of the physician. Whereas in the 1920's the doctor-patient relationship was dominated by the "class medicine" principle, Soviet writers now consider medical ethics to be above class distinctions. In 1917 "faculty vows" were abolished in all Russian universities, and now they have been reintroduced in several Soviet medical institutes. Similarly, whereas in the 1920's the first edition of the *Large Medical Encyclopedia* countenanced the practice of carrying out scientific experiments on human beings, the second edition categorically condemned those performed by Nazi doctors. The second edition also censured "mercy killings," whereas in 1929 this practice was fully condoned.[49] Finally, although the Soviet regime has eliminated the influence of religious morality on medical ethics, the present "moral code of the builders of communism" is permeated with a fundamentally humane and therefore essentially religious morality.

All these facts stand out in bold relief as evidence that efforts by Soviet doctors to embrace firm moral values have not gone unrewarded. Even though they have not achieved all their goals, and although Soviet medical ethics are heavily larded with communist propaganda, the doctors must be given credit for having achieved a tangible measure of success. The issue is far from resolved, however, and the final outcome is as yet uncertain.

---

[47] S. Utkin, *op. cit.*, p. 98.

[48] *Bolshaya meditsinskaya entsiklopediya*, 2nd ed., Vol. XXXV, Moscow, 1964, p. 838.

[49] *Trud i byt sovetskogo vracha* (The Work and Life of a Soviet Doctor), Kharkov, 1929, p. 17.

Appendix I

The Hippocratic Oath

I swear by Apollo, the Physician, and Asclepios, Hygeia and Panacea and all the gods and goddesses, that, according to my ability and judgement, I will keep this oath and this stipulation—to reckon him who taught me this Art equally dear to me as my parents, to share my substance with him, and relieve his necessities if required; to look upon his offspring in the same footing as my own brothers, and teach them this Art, if they shall wish to learn it, without fee or stipulation; and that by precept, lecture and every other mode of instruction, I will impart a knowledge of the Art to my own sons, and to those of my teachers and disciples bound by a stipulation and oath according to the law of medicine—but to none other. I will follow that system of regimen which, according to my ability and judgement, I consider for the benefit of my patients, and abstain from whatever is deleterious and mischievous. I will give no deadly medicine to any one if asked, nor suggest any such counsel; and in like manner I will not give to a woman a pessary to produce abortion. With purity and with holiness I will pass my life and practise my Art. I will not cut persons labouring under the stone, but will leave this to be done by men who are practitioners of this work. Into whatever houses I enter, I will go into them for the benefit of the sick, and will abstain from every voluntary act of mischief and corruption; and, further, from the seduction of females or males, of freemen or slaves. Whatever, in connection with my professional practice, or not in connection with it, I see or hear, in the life of men, which ought not to be spoken of abroad, I will not divulge, as reckoning that all such should be kept secret. While I continue to keep this Oath unviolated, may it be granted to me to enjoy life and the practice of the Art, respected by all men, in all times! But should I trespass and violate this Oath, may the reverse be my lot!

Appendix II

The Faculty Oath

(An oath signed by doctors when they graduated from medical schools in the former Russian Empire. See *Bulletin of the Pirogovsky Society of Russian Emigré Doctors*, Vol. I, Nr. 10, Munich, 1952, p. 9).

In accepting with deep gratitude the medical licence bestowed on me by science, and understanding the significance of the responsibilities placed upon me by my knowledge, I promise that throughout my entire life I will in no way darken the reputation of the class which I am entering.

I promise at any time to help to the best of my understanding those who come to me for aid, to sacredly guard family confidences entrusted to me and not to misuse the trust shown me. I promise to continue my study of medical science and to promote with all my strength its progress, reporting to the scientific world everything I discover. I promise not to engage in the preparation and sale of illicit medicines. I promise to be fair to my fellow doctors and not to offend them personally; however, if the good of the patient demands it, I promise to speak the truth frankly, without partiality. In important cases I promise to resort to the advice of doctors better informed and more experienced than I am; and when I am summoned for consultation, I will conscientiously do justice to their merits and endeavours.

Appendix III

Ethical Precepts

(Precepts developed by the doctors of the Darnitsky Hospital in Kiev. Translated from *Meditsinskaya gazeta*, December 18, 1962).

1. Prevention of disease is your primary duty. The present and future belong to preventive medicine.

2. The human organism is an integral system. Treat the patient as well as the disease.

3. Knowledge which is not enriched diminishes with each passing day. Acquire your knowledge in a systematic way.

4. It is harmful and dangerous to pretend to know that which you do not know. Do not be ashamed to turn to your colleagues for advice. The interests of the patient are above all else.

5. Treat the patient in the same way that you would wish to be treated if you were sick. Medicine without a few kind words will have very little or no effect at all. Care for the psychological well-being of your patient.

6. Cherish your prestige and that of your colleagues. Faith in recovery is half the battle.

7. The sufferings of the patient are a very serious matter. Treatment means to relieve pain and not to cause it.

8. The patient is not just an impersonal object of medical endeavours. Look for something actively in common with him.

9. The more people there are caring for the fate of the patient, the sooner he will recover. Take notice of the patient's relatives and friends; involve them in the care of his health.

10. Criticism is bitter medicine, but it is not poison. Do not conceal your errors and do not cover up the mistakes of your colleague. The patient's interest is at stake.

11. Be mentally alert, morally pure and physically fit. Envy, ambition, self-interest and pride are inconsistent with your profession.

12. Try to save the person's life right to the very end, so that it can be said of you: You tried every possible solution and devoted all your energies to this purpose.

Appendix IV

A Moral Code for the Builder of Communism

— Dedication to the Communist cause, love for one's Socialist Fatherland and for countries under socialism;

— conscientious labour for the good of society; he who does not work, does not eat;

— the concern of each and everyone for the preservation and augmentation of the community property;

— a deep awareness of one's public duty and an intolerance of infringements of public interests;

— cooperative and friendly mutual assistance; all for one and one for all;

— humane treatment and mutual respect among people; each one treats the other as a friend, comrade and brother;

— honesty and justice, moral purity, simplicity and modesty in one's public and private life;

— mutual respect in the family and care for the rearing of one's children;

— relentless animosity towards injustice, parasitism, dishonesty and self-seeking;

— friendship and fraternity for all peoples of the Soviet Union and intolerance of national and racial prejudices;

— relentless animosity towards the opponents of communism and the cause of peace and freedom throughout the world;

— a fraternal solidarity with the workers of all countries and with all nations.

SOURCE: *Izvestia*, July 30, 1961.

Protestant Influences
on the Outlook of the Soviet Citizen Today

William C. Fletcher

The Russian Baptist movement is one of the most important of the religious movements in the USSR. Partly because of its dynamism and zeal, partly because of its well developed religious rationale, but primarily, one suspects, because of the peculiarities of Soviet law and policy regarding the sectarian movements, the All-Union Council of Evangelical Christians-Baptists (AUCECB) is the most prominent Protestant organization in Soviet society. This paper will attempt to assess the current significance of the Baptists and the role which they may reasonably be expected to play in the society which is emerging.

It should not be understood that the AUCECB is the only representative of Protestant Christianity in the USSR. Non-Orthodox religious sects of local, regional, and even national significance abound—groups such as the Molokans, Dhukhobors, Seven Day Adventists, Pentecostals, Jehovah's Witnesses, and many, many others of greater or lesser import—but Soviet policy denies them permission to organize on a national scale, and the AUCECB is allowed and perhaps even encouraged by the state to assimilate other Protestant denominations into its ranks. There are other Protestant bodies in some of the national republics which are organized to one degree or another—Lutherans and Methodists in the Baltic states, for example—but, because their member churches are, in the main, confined to a single area, they would not seem to have as great a potential for influencing Soviet society at large as does the AUCECB.

Therefore this paper will confine itself to the Russian Baptists, for in many respects this movement may be paradigmatic for Russian Protestantism as a whole, and much of what is given below may be applicable, *mutatis mutandis*, to other Protestant groups as well.

One of the first questions to be analyzed in assessing the place of the Russian Baptist movement in the new society which is emerging in the USSR is the magnitude of its current influence. Unfortunately, this question is exceedingly difficult to evaluate from outside the Soviet Union.

Statistical data on the size of the Baptist movement are not especially valuable, and, indeed, the proper evaluation of such statistical data is one of the more perplexing tasks of Soviet lore. The accepted membership figure is around a half million[1]—figures given by members of the AUCECB range from 530,000

---

[1] Michael Bourdeaux, *Opium of the People*, London: Faber and Faber, 1965, p. 153; *Religion in the USSR*, Institute for the Study of the USSR, Munich, 1960, p. 135.

baptized members,[2] 545,000 members,[3] 550,000 members with 3,000,000 sympathizers,[4] to 600,000 members with 1,000,000 sympathizers.[5] Unfortunately, these figures have been so invariable for the past two decades and so immune to patterns of growth or decline, that one may suspect that they are round figures only, compiled, perhaps, on the basis of an even hundred members per church for however many churches are claimed at a given instant.[6] Therefore a degree of caution would seem in order when citing these figures.

Nor does an examination of the historical growth patterns of the Baptist movement offer much help. In the mid-20's Baptist claims ranged from 3,500,000[7] and 1,000,000[8] to 200,000,[9] while Soviet sources claim that during the decade following 1916 the Baptist movement lost half its membership,[10] declining from 114,652 members in 1915 to 50,124.[11] According to the Commissariat of the Interior, Evangelical Christians in 29 provinces of the RSFSR increased by 13 per cent in 1925 alone;[12] the Baptist movement suffered decreases of from 10.9 per cent to "almost three times" and "four times" in 1929–1932 in given regions,[13] and for the rest of the 30's their decline was precipitate.[14] By the mid-30's they were reduced to 250,000 according to Soviet sources,[15] and their decline continued to such a point that in 1942, one year after the German invasion of the USSR, Baptist leaders could claim only 40,000 followers.[16] The movement revived in post-war years,[17] however, increasing to 400,000 by 1948,[18] and reaching the

---

[2] S. D. Bailey, "Religious Boom in Russia," *Christian Century*, Chicago, No. 75, March 12, 1958, p. 304.

[3] Josef Nordenhaug, ed., *The Truth that Makes Men Free* (official report of the Eleventh Congress, Baptist World Alliance), Nashville, Tenn: Broadman Press, 1966, p. 559.

[4] Walter Kolarz, "Religious Believers in Soviet Russia," *Listener*, London, Jan. 29, 1959, p. 199.

[5] Charles Foltz, Jr., "Religion in Russia Today: A First Hand Report," *U. S. News and World Report*, Washington D. C., Vol. LVI, No. 6, February 10, 1964, p. 57.

[6] Walter Kolarz, *Religion in the Soviet Union*, London: Macmillan, 1962, pp. 286, 305.

[7] James Henry Rushbrooke, *Some Chapters of European Baptist History*, London: Kingsgate Press, 1929, pp. 11–12; P. A. Yefimov, "Overcoming Baptism in the USSR, 1923–1929," in *Yezhegodnik muzeya istorii religii i ateizma*, Moscow-Leningrad: Academy of Sciences of the USSR, Vol. VI, 1962, pp. 167–168, quoting *Bezbozhnik*, January 3, 1930.

[8] *Ibid.*, quoting *Baptist*, London, No. 6, 1926, pp. 11–12.

[9] *Ibid.*, p. 168, quoting the World Congress of Baptists, 1928 (in Canada).

[10] *Ibid.*, pp. 164–165.

[11] *Ibid.*, p. 168.

[12] A. Veshchikov, "Milestones of a Great Journey," *Nauka i religiya*, No. 11, November 1962. English translation in *Religion in Communist-Dominated Areas* (hereafter RCDA), New York, December 24, 1962, p. 5.

[13] *Sovremennoye sektantstvo* (Contemporary Sectarianism), Vol. IX of the series *Voprosy istorii religii i ateizma*, Moscow: Academy of Sciences of the USSR, 1961, p. 29.

[14] *Ibid.*, pp. 29–30.

[15] *Kolarz, op. cit.*, p. 286, citing Putintsev, *Politicheskaya rol i taktika sekt* (The Political Role and Tactics of the Sects), Moscow, 1935, p. 449.

[16] *Baptist Times*, July 9, 1942.

[17] *Sovremennoye sektantstvo, op. cit.*, pp. 30, 124–125; E. F. Muravev and Yu. V. Dmitrev, "Concreteness in Studying and Overcoming Religious Survivals," *Voprosy filosofii*, No. 3, March, 1961, p. 64. English translation in *Soviet Review*, New York, No. 2, July, 1961, pp. 42, 43; also in *Current Digest of the Soviet Press* (hereafter CDSP), New York, Vol. XIII, No. 20, June 14, 1961, pp. 3–7.

[18] *Bratsky Vestnik* (hereafter *BV*), No. 1, 1948, pp. 6–7.

half-million mark thereafter. According to results of a field study published by the Academy of Sciences of the USSR in 1961, conservative estimates of the then current overall strength of the Baptist movement show a decline of four and one half times from the 1928 level.[19]

Considering the disparateness of the data, perhaps the following statement gives a good picture of the usefulness of such evidence regarding the Baptists:

> The development of sects of Western origin, whose appearance in Russia dates back to the end of the nineteenth century, is also on a declining curve. A. I. Klibanov showed the degeneration of such sects as the Evangelical Christians-Baptists, the Pentecostals, and the Seventh-Day Adventists. However, the Voronezh Baptist community has grown in postwar years, which calls for intensified ideological work. True, the sects named are characterized by shrinking numbers, a considerable increase in the average age of the members, a preponderance of women, and a sharp drop in the number of workers, collective farmers and employees.[20]

Perhaps a more useful index of the strength of the Baptist movement is to be found in the attitude of the regime towards the Baptists. The hostility of the regime towards the Baptists is out of all proportion to a movement whose adherents, according to official figures, number under one quarter of one per cent of the total population. Soviet policy towards the Baptists has already received adequate documentation,[21] so this paper will not go into great detail.

The current anti-religious campaign has been especially intense with regard to the Baptists, and the pressures applied by the state have increased dramatically during the past half-dozen years. The measures applied against the Baptists range from such customary annoyances as job discrimination,[22] and lack of adequate printed materials,[23] to more crippling limitations. Places of worship have presented an especial problem during the past few years. On rare occasion the Baptists have been able to purchase houses for worship service,[24] but at extremely high prices.[25] Many church buildings have been declared closed, leaving the congregation without a place of worship,[26] thus adding poignancy to the doctrine that God's temple is the heart, not a building made with hands.[27]

---

[19] *Sovremennoye sektantstvo, op. cit.*, p. 23.

[20] I. A. Malakhova, "Historians Are Studying Present-Day Religious Movements," *Istoriya SSSR*, No. 2, March-April 1961, p. 233. English translation from *CDSP*, Vol. XII, No. 17, May 24, 1961, p. 15.

[21] E. g., Kolarz, *op. cit.*, pp. 301, 321; Bourdeaux, *op. cit.*, pp. 154—169; J. C. Pollack, *The Christians from Siberia*, London: Hodder and Stoughton, 1964, *passim*.

[22] *Izvestia*, December 11, 1963; V. Stepanenko, "Four Wasted Years," *Komsomolskaya Pravda*, March 25, 1965. English translation in *RCDA*, April 30, 1965, pp. 63—64.

[23] Ya. I. Zhidkov, "Over the Land of Siberia" *BV*, No. 2, 1963. English translation in *RCDA*, December 23, 1963, p. 245; as a further example, only three issues of the normally bi-monthly *BV* appeared in 1965.

[24] E. g., *BV*, No. 4, 1964, p. 80.

[25] M. S. Voronovich, comp., *Pravda o sektantakh* (The Truth about the Sectarians), Vladivostok: *Primorskoye Knizhnoye Izdatelstvo*, 1958, p. 129; *The Beleaguered Fortress*, New York: Information Center on Soviet Affairs, 1963, p. 22.

[26] Voronovich, *op. cit.*, p. 127; Zhidkov, *op. cit.*, p. 244.

[27] A. D. B., "Temples of God," *BV*, No. 3, 1964, pp. 36—37. English translation in *RCDA*, January 15, 1965, p. 2.

Other congregations have had to move to relatively inaccessible locations far from the centre of town.[28] And of course a vast number of Baptists have been denied permission to register, which renders any gatherings illegal (see below).

A considerable number of court trials of Baptists have appeared during the current anti-religious campaign, with three to five years as the normal sentence (under Article 227 of the Criminal Code).[29] This is of course by no means a novelty in the lives of the Baptists, for many of those now serving as leaders in the AUCECB suffered similar penalties during the pre-war period.[30]

Perhaps the most telling indication of the seriousness with which the regime views the Baptist movement is to be found in the known cases of deprivation of parental rights for religious reasons. This measure, whereby parents guilty of teaching religion to their children are convicted of spiritually crippling their children and the children are then removed to state (and hence atheistic) boarding schools,[31] has been applied most frequently against the more radical non-Orthodox groups.[32] However, the dramatic evidence left at the U.S. Embassy in January, 1963, which included letters from children in such state boarding schools,[33] came from a group which called themselves "Evangelical Christians,"[34] implying that they may have been Baptists who had been denied permission to register and worship legally. As recently as 1966 the following, which may be an oblique reference to denial of parent rights, appeared.

> The facts show that in re-educating believers all the forms of individual work are not yet being used. It is precisely this which can explain the fact that Anna Neplokh remains to this day in the ranks of the Baptists. True, *it has been possible to save Anna's children from this. They have been put in the Disensk boarding school.* But how many like Anna still remain in the region![35]

It is in the reaction of the Baptists to the renewal of pressure that the most important gauge of the movement's potential influence in society is to be found. This reaction is certainly one of the most dramatic and perhaps one of the most important episodes in the recent history of religion in the USSR.

The reaction was expressed in schism. A continuing problem for the AUCECB is the fissiparous tendency which is inherent in any such religious organization.

---

[28] Zhidkov, *op. cit.*, p. 245; Bourdeaux, *op. cit.*, p. 154.

[29] A. Kafarov, "False Prophets," *Bakinsky rabochy*, April 7, 1963, translated in *RCDA*, May 27, 1963, p. 85 (see also *RCDA's* editorial comment on this article, p. 83); E. Popok, "Obscurantists with Tape Recorders," *Sovetskaya kultura*, February 3, 1962, p. 4, translated in *CDSP*, Vol. XIV, No. 7, March 14, 1962, p. 40; *The Beleaguered Fortress, op. cit.*, p. 14.

[30] Zhidkov, *op. cit.*, p. 244; *BV*, No. 6, 1963, p. 39.

[31] D. Konstantinov, "Further Blows at Religion," *Bulletin*, Institute for the Study of the USSR, November, 1962, p. 53; cf. *Kazakhstanskaya pravda*, June 24, 1964.

[32] *Turkmenskaya iskra*, September, 1962, translation in *RCDA*, March 18, 1963, pp. 12–13; *Pravda*, October 3, 1964, translation in *CDSP*, October 28, 1964, p. 32.

[33] *Newsweek*, New York, January 28, 1963, p. 45.

[34] *Los Angeles Times*, January 4, 1963; cf. Harry Willets, "De-opiating the Masses," *Problems of Communism*, Washington D. C., November-December, 1964, p. 37.

[35] F. Agafonov, "Without Proper Sharpness and Aggressiveness," *Kommunist Belorusii*, No. 2, February, 1966, p. 68, italics mine.

Separatist movements the world over have always had an inclination to break apart into ever smaller groups. Without the strong tradition of ecclesiastical discipline which marks the more highly organized approaches to religious life, movements such as the Baptists, with their deep distrust of institutional organization, are continually plagued by splinter groups breaking away from the organized movement. In Soviet conditions this difficulty is increased by state policy, which allows the multitudes of baptistic and related groups only a single legal organization. Thus, the AUCECB was originally formed in 1944 from the two distinct bodies of Baptists and Evangelical Christians, each with its own history and its own seminal organization, and a year after its formation the AUCECB came to include the Pentecostals as well. In 1963 the Mennonites were invited to join,[36] which would render the problem of overcoming centrifugal tendencies even more acute.

The results, of course, have been a succession of schismatic movements.[37] Within a year after the inclusion of the Pentecostals, the majority of the Pentecostals left the AUCECB.[38] A more serious wave of schismatic movements, however, was occasioned by the great emancipation of convicts from the labour camps in the mid-fifties, when the regime's de-emphasis of the secret police apparatus resulted in a vast reduction of the penal labour force:

> After the return into the societies in 1953–54 of several old workers, who for a long time had not been participants in the complicated and laborious work for unification of the three streams of differing origin in faith, and who maintained their old negative views on collaboration of Evangelical Christians, Baptists and Pentecostals, they began their attempts at organizing their own personal groupings, such groupings as the so-called "Pure Baptists," or the groupings of the so-called "Evangelical Christians-Perfectionists," and the like. But despite their activity it was difficult for them to go against the will of God.[39]

Judging from the scant data currently available it would seem that of the two the more serious threat to the AUCECB was the "Pure Baptist" movement. Permission to preach had been limited by the AUCECB to the ordained pastor and his three-man executive staff, in what would seem an obvious attempt to maintain some control over the proceedings at worship services. In an attempt to overcome this limitation, which was doubtless imposed on the AUCECB by the state, the "Pure Baptists" demanded literal fulfillment of the doctrine of the priesthood of all believers, holding that every member of the church should be ordained to preach by the "laying on of hands."

> In the Ukraine we were met with the followers of so-called "Pure Baptism." The followers of "Pure Baptism" began to carry on their work in the societies of Donetsk, Lugansk, Zaporozhe, Dnepropetrovsk, and several other oblasts. At first they succeeded in achieving some temporary successes. Several groups of "Pure

---

[36] *BV*, No. 6, 1964, pp. 3, 43.
[37] E. g., *BV*, No. 4, 1962, translation in *RCDA*, May 6, 1963, p. 62.
[38] *BV*, No. 6, 1963, p. 35.
[39] *Ibid.*, p. 21.

Baptists" were founded. Their main teaching was opposition to the unity already achieved. They taught that it was obligatory for all brothers and sisters of the Evangelical Christians to receive the laying on of hands, they condemned receiving brothers and sisters from the Pentecostals into our ranks, and they condemned the leadership of our Union for the unity achieved, considering this an impure business... [40]

According to anti-religious sources, "the so-called 'Pure Paptists' demand a more active and diversified religious propaganda and the introduction of a greater number of new members into their sect."[41]

Apparently the churches of the AUCECB were able to overcome the schismatic movement. The following is an illustration of one of the arguments which could be employed in resisting such movements:

"Once," said a brother [from Belorussia] "a brother came up to me in our society and said, 'We have to create some sort of small group for cleansing the church.' 'But we have no such instruction in God's Word!' I answered the brother." Matt. 3 : 12 answers this question for us. The blade is in the hand of the Lord, dear friends, only He Himself can apply it, but He never entrusts it to us....If He had entrusted it to anyone else, then one might dare to say that many unfortunate consequences would have followed.[42]

Repentant "Pure Baptists" have told their stories in the pages of the AUCECB periodical, *Bratsky Vestnik*, [43] and

today almost all the groups of "pure Baptists" in the Ukraine have dispersed, with the exception of four small groups in Donetsk Oblast. These groups have no influence whatsoever in our societies.[44]

The "Evangelical Christians-Perfectionists" had a similar history. The movement

began first of all in Sumsky Oblast, where the so-called teachings on perfectionism arose; a certain Kornienko spread this teaching. However, today this group has dispersed almost entirely and exists as small groups of less than 10 people only in two or three places. Kornienko, the initiator of this teaching, at the present time has no influence whatsoever in our societies.[45]

We find articles corroborating these data in the anti-religious press: allegedly seeking easy living and money, "the religious merchants invent their own 'teachings' and create new 'sects,' calling themselves 'renewers,' 'perfectionists,' etc."[46]

These schisms occurred during a time when the anti-religious engines of the state were relatively idle, and apparently had little lasting effect on the life of the

---

[40] *Ibid.*, pp. 35–36.
[41] *Kafarov, op. cit.*, p. 83.,
[42] *BV*, No. 6, 1964, p. 46.
[43] *Ibid.*, No. 6, 1963, pp. 39–40.
[44] *Ibid.*, p. 36, cf. p. 21.
[45] *Ibid.*, p. 35.
[46] *Izvestia*, October 6, 1960. Condensed translation in *CDSP*, November 2, 1960, p. 34.

church. The schismatic movement which arose during the current campaign, however, was far more serious:

> New, stronger attempts to divide our brotherhood were undertaken by the so-called "Initiative Group" beginning in August, 1961. The causes of these attempts are known to all our brotherhood and we will not take time for a detailed exposition of them.[47]

This statement was made at the All-Union Convention of the AUCECB, held in Moscow, October 15–17, 1963. The Convention was called precisely in response to the challenge of the Initiative Group, and therefore the above passage must be understood as an understatement. A more illuminating picture of the seriousness of the challenge may be derived from the following statement at the Convention:

> In the past two years in the Ukraine we have lived through new attempts at dividing our brotherhood in several of our societies. These attempts arise from the followers of the so-called "Initiative Group." Although in several societies in individual oblasts of the Ukraine groups of supporters of the "Initiative Group" have been founded, nevertheless the overwhelming majority of our societies are preserving unity and supporting our fraternal union of the AUCECB. One should note that in a whole series of oblasts of the Ukraine the "Initiative Group" has not attained success and has not founded its groups in a single society. Such oblasts are: Chernovits, Zakarpatsk, Ternopol, Volyn, Rovensk and others, and in several oblasts such for example as Khersonese, Nikolaev, Dnepropetrovsk, Lvov, Poltava, and others, there are two or three groups in all. The influence of the "Initiative Group" in the main is in Donetsk, Kharkov, Lugansk, and a few other oblasts.
>
> The work of the followers of the "Initiative Group" at first was not understood and several believers, not going into the substance of the matter, did not see anything bad in the calls to fasting and prayer for the cleansing of the church. But many quickly understood that the cleansing of the church for which they called was in fact the division of the church and was a matter unpleasing to the Lord.
>
> Dear brothers! We should not forget that for many years the children of God in our country thirsted for unity, prayed for it, and waited for it. And then in 1944–45, the Lord gave us unity. And how we should thank the Lord for this. Can it be that now, at the summons of the "Initiative Group," we should again start on the path of division instead of strengthening unity and founding peace in the churches? Can it be that the Lord does not call us to unity? Many churches understood the dangerous work of the "Initiative Group" which leads to division, and did not go along with them.[48]

The schism apparently began in response to an instruction issued by the AUCECB to its senior presbyters ordering them to avoid preaching when requested to do so by churches in their territory and to instruct their churches not to baptize candidates under thirty years of age, and no longer to seek new converts but to concentrate exclusively on those who are already members of

---

[47] *BV*, No. 6, 1963, pp. 21–22.
[48] *Ibid.*, p. 36.

the church.[49] This order was as diametrically opposed to the evangelical élan of the Baptists as the contemporaneous order issued by the Moscow Patriarchate placing all parish affairs in the hands of a lay council was opposed to the tradition of Orthodoxy, and, like it, could only have been initiated by the state in an attempt to impede the work of the churches.

It was this order which provided the focal point for the dissident elements in the Baptist movement. The opposition grew, to such a degree that

> from November 29 to December 2, 1961, consultations were held by the AUCECB and senior presbyters in connection with the appearance of activity of the so-called "Initiative Group," which was led by A. F. Prokofev and G. K. Kryuchkov. At this consultation, in addition to the members of the AUCECB and auditing commission, 12 senior presbyters participated.[50]

The leader of the movement, Prokofev, was subsequently arrested and given a five-year sentence,[51] but the movement continued, presumably under the leadership of Kryuchkov.

The Initiative Group grew rapidly, and soon reached sufficient strength to cause some of those connected with it to dispatch letters of protest to the authorities. George Bailey cites one example of a letter to Khrushchev protesting against injustice and discrimination.[52] Such protests are contrary to a cardinal policy of the AUCECB, which has never publicly opposed any action of the state regardless of how detrimental such action may be to the church; in return, it has been allowed limited freedom to operate.

Perhaps because of its recognition of the seriousness of such challenges and also because of its intimate knowledge of the very real threat they represented to the delicate balance of church-state relations, the AUCECB reacted rather strongly:

> We caution all our brothers and sisters against various sorts of letters, which, representing attempts to place our brotherhood in an aggravated position with the rulership and government of our country, are dangerous and threatening for the entire work of the Lord in our country. This not only is threatening for our entire brotherhood, it also contradicts the whole spirit of the Gospel and the teaching of our Lord Jesus Christ.[53]

But the very fact that such protests appeared at all may suggest that one of the points at issue in the schism was dissatisfaction with the AUCECB leadership policy of acceptance of the political actions of the regime.

To judge by the reactions of the AUCECB, the Initiative Group must soon have reached sufficient proportions to allow it directly to challenge the old

---

[49] George Bailey, "Religion in the Soviet Union," *Reporter*, New York, July 16, 1964, p. 28; cf. *Uspekhi sovremennoy nauki i religiya* (Contemporary Science's Successes and Religion), Moscow: Academy of Sciences of the USSR, 1961, p. 28; Muravev and Dmitrev, *op. cit.*, *Soviet Review* translation, p. 53.

[50] *BV*, No. 6, 1963, p. 13.

[51] *Sovetskaya Moldaviya*, January 27, 1963.

[52] Bailey, *loc. cit.*

[53] *BV*, No. 6, 1963, p. 52.

leadership. There are direct hints that revision of the by-laws of the Baptist Union was demanded, and, indeed, it is far from impossible that the Initiative Group began to demand that some form of constituent assembly be held:

> It is no secret that in our brotherhood there are several questions which evoke different opinions. We in the Ukraine two years ago set before the AUCECB the question of calling an All-Union Convention of the ECB in order to study those questions which evoke different opinions.[54]

Such a conference was indeed held by the AUCECB in October of 1963. National conferences are such a rarity in the AUCECB that the very fact that it was held suggests serious reasons behind its convocation. Particularly significant is the fact that it was held at the height of an anti-religious campaign, the intensity of which was far from waning (the famous call by Ilichev for further intensification of the campaign came less than three months later). For religious bodies to be allowed to hold national conferences of any sort at such a time is unheard of, particularly when, as we shall see, the conference in question resulted in what would appear to be an alleviation of the stringent control over the member churches. Thus the holding of the Convention of 1963 would seem to imply an exceedingly serious challenge by the Initiative Group.

The major business of the Convention was revision of the rules of the AUCECB:

> As is well known, the Provisions of the AUCECB have changed twice since 1944: in 1948 and in 1960.

> The Provisions of the AUCECB of 1960 from the very beginning were not considered final and permanent, and therefore they were referred for discussion to our societies, to which the AUCECB, as is well known, twice sent letters accordingly, with the request to send their observations and intelligent suggestions, for the purpose of reviewing and changing these Provisions of the AUCECB as time passes.

> After this, very interesting suggestions and good wishes for making changes in the Provisions of the AUCECB were received from many of our societies.

> Considering all this and the emergence of new possibilities for us, the AUCECB now invites the Convention to consideration and ratification of revised Provisions of the AUCECB, which we will now call the Statutes of the Union of Evangelical Christians-Baptists.[55]

Among the desired modifications expressed during the convention were reflections of dissatisfaction with the 1961 instruction to senior presbyters, contrasting the great emphasis of the AUCECB on foreign affairs with its inadequate attention to the internal needs of the church.

> Our future desire for the new constitution of the AUCECB is as follows: at the proper time to give attention to the urgent questions of the societies as they arise, which cannot be decided locally; to exercise stricter supervision over the work of individual senior presbyters, that their work should not evoke criticism on

[54] *Ibid.*, p. 37.
[55] *Ibid.*, p. 42.

70

the part of individual societies served by them; that their work might be work which strengthens unity.

From the paper of the AUCECB it is evident that the AUCECB has attended insufficiently to the inner work dealt with in the paper itself. Therefore the AUCECB in future should give serious attention to this and elect workers who might give exclusive attention to internal work. We hope that these measures will help to remove the division of opinion...[56]

The revised Statutes of the AUCECB would seem to represent a partial victory for the Initiative Group. Unfortunately, space does not permit a detailed examination of the Statutes, but a few of the more interesting features may be noted.[57]

Perhaps most important is Paragraph 17, which defines the church as composed of believers "who have reached full adulthood and who have received baptism by water according to [their] faith." No mention is made of age limitation or of a trial period prior to baptism, which would seem to indicate a withdrawal of the injunction in the 1961 instruction.

Paragraph 19 repeats the clause that the churches meet in houses supplied by the state, but adds that rented quarters may be used. Paragraph 20 stipulates that services may be held on Sundays and major holidays, but also "on weekdays at the discretion of the [local] church." The Lord's supper is also to be celebrated "at the discretion of the church" according to Paragraph 21. Paragraph 23 removes the limitation that leadership of worship services be confined to the three-man executive in case of the pastor's illness, allowing members of the church council or "preachers of the church" to be appointed, and Paragraph 24 allows any member of the church to preach. Paragraph 26 removes the stipulation that choir directors be members of the church. All of these stipulations would seem to represent changes in the direction of greater freedom of action for the local churches through the lessening of the degree of control which can be exercised by the central leadership.

Paragraph 3 states that the leaders of the AUCECB are to be elected by simple majority of voices of representatives of the local churches, which would seem to represent a concession to democratization of the leadership. However, Paragraph 7 stipulates that Senior Presbyters are appointed by the AUCECB leadership, rather than elected by the local churches.

Thus, the work of the Convention represented a partial concession to the Initiative Group, an attempt to heal the schism by giving in to some, but not to all, of their demands.

The participants in the Convention were not so sanguine as to suppose that this partial accommodation would fully satisfy all the dissidents. The work of the AUCECB "has deficiencies, they say. I say to this: the sun in heaven also has spots, but it continues to remain the sun and gives light to all."[58] But it was

---

[56] *Ibid.*, p. 37.

[57] The Revised Statutes of the AUCECB may be found in *BV*, No. 6, 1963, pp. 43—47.

[58] *Ibid.*, p. 40.

hoped that sufficient had been granted to heal the rupture. "We should depart hence with the balm of comfort and peace for our churches, since there is no longer any reason for disputing and accusing one another."[59]

Immediate steps were taken to gain maximum effect from the Convention in the local churches.

The All-Union Convention considers it essential to turn with a special Fraternal Epistle to all children of God who are outside the unity—with a call to remove all the reasons which may hinder our full unity, that by all of us may be fulfilled the will of our Lord Jesus, expressed in His words of the high priestly prayer [for unity].[60]

The Epistle contained the following points of interest:

First of all we examined the multilateral activity which the All-Union Council of Evangelical Christians-Baptists conducts. This activity is expressed:
. . . .
5. . . . in intercession for registration of churches, in intercession for preserving and improving houses of prayer; in defending the rights and interests of individual churches and presbyters before higher authorities;
. . . .
8. In the very great work of preserving unity in our great Evangelical Baptist brotherhood, and we should note that in spite of the numerous attempts to disrupt the unity of our beloved brotherhood, it steadfastly preserves this unity and will preserve it in accordance with the will of our divine High Priest Jesus Christ, Who says, "That they all may be one" (John 17 : 21).[61]

Concurrently, Senior Presbyters were to make more frequent visits to the churches of their areas in order to help overcome the schisms.[62]

These measures enjoyed partial success. I. I. Motorin, for example, on a visit to Western Siberia, gave helpful explanations of the purity of the Gospel truth and about the correct relationship to the civil laws of the country.[63] Similarly, "The church in Tashkent for a long time suffered from division. The Lord blessed the work of the presbyter, brother Fadyukhin, and more than 400 members returned to the church for work together."[64] It is interesting that despite the great seriousness of the schism within his church, no mention of it appears in Fadyukhin's report to the Convention of 1963.[65]

The work of the Convention did not enjoy complete success, however. A year later the AUCECB was still bothered with unregistered groups,[66] and the schism was still very much of a live problem:

[59] Ibid., p. 50.
[60] Ibid., p. 42.
[61] Ibid., p. 51.
[62] Ibid., p. 42; cf. BV, No. 6, 1964, p. 74.
[63] Ibid., No. 4, 1964, p. 79.
[64] Ibid., p. 71.
[65] Ibid., No. 6, 1963, p. 40.
[66] Ibid., No. 6, 1964, pp. 41—43.

Unfortunately, it is necessary to say that the enemy of men's souls can never look calmly at the unity of the children of God and always tries to scatter them like wheat. He has not been dozing with respect to our dear brotherhood and one must say with grief that some brothers and sisters in our churches busy themselves with sowing not the seeds of peace and love but the bad seeds of enmity and separation.

. . . .

We are sure that those few groups of believers standing aside from our one Union will realize that there are no grounds for separation and we all together can praise our Lord with joy.[67]

Nor were references to the continuation of the schismatic movement especially subtle:

I do not wish to go into detail in order not to cast reproach on anybody and not to have it taken that some believers will be upheld by the regulations accepted at the Convention while others will have another opinion, but I wish to say that we have considered how to make of two opinions one and in which manner to resolve the barrier which consists of a certain enmity, a misunderstanding caused by preconceived thoughts.[68]

Thus one can imagine that the ranks of the Initiative Group have thinned somewhat as a result of the Convention, but it would not appear that their power has been drastically reduced. The anti-religious press, which devotes relatively little space to the inner disputes of the AUCECB, noted the existence of a schismatic group in 1964,[69] and *Pravda* specifically mentioned the continuing activities of the Initiative Group in 1966.[70]

The most convincing evidence of the continuing seriousness of the schism is to be found in a letter of protest from Barnaul and Kulanda in Siberia, dated February 2, 1964. This letter gives direct evidence that the schism was considered serious not only by the church but by the state as well.

We give an excerpt from the judgement rendered by the Altai District Court in Case No. 142, where it is stated that a group of Baptists conducted meetings illegally and under unsanitary conditions, and brought young people and minors into the sectarian group; under the guise of "cleansing" it (the group) conducted propaganda against the AUCECB and its statutes, and maintained contact with similar illegal groups, and more allegations of the same kind.

In the concluding accusation is written: "The guilt of the accused persons is confirmed by the following evidence. As regards reactionary activity harmful to society, such and such persons (names given) declared that the group of sectarians... analyzed various Biblical texts, permitted arbitrary and incorrect interpretation, criticized and did not accept the new constitution of the AUCECB."

There you have all the evidence given regarding reactionary activity harmful to society. One might think that the witnesses were members of the Holy Synod,

---

[67] *Ibid.*, p. 3—4.
[68] *Ibid.*, p. 48.
[69] *Komsomolets Uzbekistana*, February 2, 1964.
[70] *Pravda*, February 19, 1966.

people with higher theological education, well versed in Biblical truths and called to defend the impeccability of Biblical truths. But not at all!

Dear Brothers and Sisters: The fact is that the world cannot permit the illegally acquired right atheistically to interpret the Bible to us, to force us into the church of its servants, to dig into their "constitution" (statutes) and then to take vengeance on all the servants who have been appointed by the Lord and elected by the Church. But they do this very simply. Since in the Civil Code there is no article against incorrect interpretation of the Bible, the Prosecutor called it harmful to society and reactionary activity, and thereby put the "incorrect" interpretation of the Bible and criticism of the constitution of the AUCECB under Article 227 of the Civil Code. The Altai Court did the same, and so it is done by other courts all over the country.

. . . .

...They condemn us not for evil deeds or for breaking the law but for good deeds, for non-recognition of the AUCECB and its "constitution" which destroy the church, but which is of such advantage to the courts for the condemnation of the faithful that they continue to render judgement on the basis of the "constitution" even though it has been "rejected." The judges of this world condemn the children of God because the AUCECB has destroyed the church and its true servants in the world, in the same way as the High Priests, scribes and Pharisees betrayed Jesus Christ to Pilate.

Such is the true image of the AUCECB. Hundreds of brothers and sisters suffer in prison and exile because of the AUCECB. The courts, with full force, support the AUCECB, and they accuse and condemn all who do not support the AUCECB.[71]

The clear implication, therefore, is that the Convention of 1963 was an action which enjoyed the full support of the state, and that the state has subsequently made use of the work of the Convention in attempting to overcome the schismatic movement by forcible measures.

It would seem, then, that the continuing history of the schism led by the Initiative Group gives dramatic and incontrovertible evidence of the great power inherent in the Baptist movement in Soviet society. Protest within the Baptist movement has demonstrably been of sufficient impact to cause the state to modify its policy toward it. That a clandestine, illegal, underground religious movement has succeeded in forcing the state to concede, if only in part, to its demands is of great significance. The only similar recent case which comes to mind would be the protests surrounding the attempt to close the Pochaevskaya Lavra, protests which have apparently succeeded in keeping the Lavra open. However, these protests concerned a specific event and were supported by relatively massive public demonstrations in the West, whereas the Initiative Group's protest appeared to have been widespread, directed against a national policy and, significantly, completely without public support from the West. The protest's successes apparently were in no way due to any public expressions of concern from abroad.

---

[71] Translated text of the letter may be found in *RCDA*, September 30, 1964, pp. 122–125.

Coming as it did during an intensive anti-religious drive, this successful protest indicates the strength of the Baptist movement. Resistance to state imposed policy within the Baptist churches was evidently too powerful to be overcome without reversion to the methods of outright force employed against religion in the pre-war period. The fact that the protest of the Initiative Group has continued despite the partial accommodation allowed by the state, and the fact that the state has thus far been unwilling to revert to the full-scale terror of the early Stalin period in combatting its influence, would seem to suggest that the Baptist movement will continue to exercise an effective influence on society for some time to come.

If this be true, then it would seem worthwhile to examine what sort of influence the Baptists may be expected to exercise in society, to derive a profile of the type of person who would be attracted to the Baptist movement.

Michael Bourdeaux was much impressed by the vitality, sincerity and courage of the Baptists,[72] and found himself wondering:

> If I had a Russian friend who was a potential convert to Christianity, would I introduce him first to the Orthodox Church or to the Baptist?...In most instances, taking everything into consideration ,I would probably advise a potential convert to go to the Baptist Church.[73]

This view, that Russian Baptists are natural competitors with Orthodoxy in the struggle for men's souls, is occasionally shared by Soviet commentators as well:

> One lecturer in his outline of the tasks of an individual worker with believers said this: "We succeeded in re-educating one old lady: she left the Baptist sect and now is a member of the Russian Orthodox Church." He sincerely believed that this was a success of anti-religious work.[74]

At least when judging this situation from the outside, it would not appear that this juxtaposition of Baptism with Orthodoxy is especially valid, for the two forms of Christianity would seem to appeal to two different types of people. Orthodoxy, with its mysterious tranquillity, with its quiet beauty and aesthetic appeal, with its calm, relatively unquestioning acceptance of the person without requiring of him energetic application of any particular tenet of the faith, accepting the person for what he is rather than for what he does, might exert a very strong appeal on someone who had seen the energetic illusions of youth evaporate in a world which does not, after all, change into Utopia overnight. A person whose ambitions had finally been crushed by the relatively inflexible environment of life (and not everyone, after all, can reach the pinnacle of success in the USSR—or anywhere else for that matter) might find the quiet mystery of Russian Orthodoxy mightily attractive.

---

[72] Bourdeaux, *op. cit.*, pp. 151—172.

[73] *Ibid.*, p. 171.

[74] A. Valentinov, "The Primer of Materialism—Notes of a Propaganda Worker," *Komsomolskaya pravda*, June 14, 1963. Translation from *RCDA*, September 9, 1963, p. 164.

Russian Orthodoxy is also the benefactor of a thousand-year identification with Russia, and thus could be expected to have great appeal for those in whom the flame of patriotism burns bright. The Russian Baptists, who with very brief exceptions have always been on the fringes of Russian society, and who take pride in the inclusion of Russians, Ukrainians, Belorussians, Latvians, Estonians, Lithuanians, Germans, Georgians, Armenians, Hungarians, Moldavians, Jews, Chuvash and other nationalities in their membership[75] could scarcely hope to compete with Orthodoxy in attracting Russians of patriotic motivation.

It is perhaps for such reasons as these that the anti-religious propagandists often consider the Baptists a threat which in some ways is more dangerous than Orthodoxy:

> One can often hear even these words: "It is not such a tragedy that some old men and women go to church. Sectarians—those are dangerous people and one must fight against them, but other believers will not disturb us."[76]

And indeed, there are strong hints of a practical ecumenism within the Baptist movement itself:

> Among rank and file believers we did not find theological disputes and often rank and file followers of various sects maintain bonds with one another. The Baptist Sukharev visited the Adventists. He considers this religion the more righteous in some particulars: "On Sunday we bake and boil but they prepare on Friday and on Saturday they eat everything cold. Well, take me, I eat and then go to the meeting. They never eat before the meeting. They are more righteous."[77]

Nor are the Orthodox excluded from the incipient ecumenicity. Taking as an example the case of a Baptist girl whose devout Orthodox grandmother had died, one of the leaders of the AUCECB stated:

> In every Christian Church there are members of the Universal Church of Christ, that is, believers with fervent hearts....If the grandmother shone with the light of love, meekness, humility and patience, this is a valid sign that she loved Christ and therefore belonged to the one Universal Church of Christ. The granddaughter and grandmother were one on the main point: they both loved Christ. But the granddaughter understood certain questions more deeply, on these questions she was convinced differently from the grandmother. And therefore the form of worship of God by the granddaughter should be somewhat different from that of the grandmother.[78]

Such remarks as these would suggest an awareness within the Baptist movement that it is quite possible that they and the Orthodox may play complementary, rather than competitive, roles in the highly pluralistic society which seems to accompany the technological revolution. It is doubtful whether any single Christian group could minister with complete success to all types of people within a complex society, and hence it may be a more correct analysis to suppose

---

[75] *BV*, No. 6, 1963, p. 22.
[76] Valentinov, *loc. cit.*
[77] *Sovremennoye sektantstvo, op. cit.*, p. 140.
[78] *BV*, No. 6, 1964, p. 35.

that Baptists and Orthodox are really allies rather than competitors in influencing society. The Baptists are competitors, not chiefly with the Orthodox, but with another element in Soviet society.

For this reason, an analysis of some of the major aspects of the Baptist rationale would seem to offer some help in determining the type of person who would be attracted by the movement. The following brief summary will attempt to illustrate some of these aspects, not in order to draw a theological picture of the Baptist approach, but in order to illustrate some of the points of appeal of the Baptist framework.

The Baptists have an easily comprehensible, rationally oriented world view. The basic tenets of the faith can be mastered in outline form in a relatively short time by a person of average intelligence. In this regard the Baptist approach differs from that of Russian Orthodoxy, which tends to elude the grasp entirely when one tries to understand it in purely rational, explicable terms. Thus the Baptist faith could be expected to appeal to that person who desires an understandable, intellectually satisfying rationale of life. (It should be noted, however, that Baptist doctrine is by no means completely consistent and without contradiction, so it might prove ultimately deficient for the person who insists on absolute rational consistency.)

Furthermore, the Baptist approach is dogmatically oriented, seeking guidelines for every aspect of life in a collection of sacrosanct writ. The Baptists affirm as one of their "basic principles":

> We deeply believe that all the Books of Holy Scripture are inspired by God (II Peter 1 : 21). The Word of God is the single rule and measure in all questions of our faith and conduct.[79]

The Baptists have a strong strain of determinism in their approach, found in the Calvinistic inclination of the movement. "What Baptism accepted from Calvinism is the teaching about predestination."[80]

> Since he does not contain in himself any positive initiative, man, according to the Baptist religion, is deprived of freedom of the will and of the possibility of purposeful activity.
>
> "From the beginning of the age" and "to the end of the age" Baptism teaches, God ordained who in the changing of human inclinations would be "elect" and "saved," who would be "condemned" and "lost." This divine predestination is unchangeable and unknowable.[81]

This deterministic element can be a rather effective adjunct to a movement's ability to satisfy its adherents. It allows members to feel that they are part of an inevitable process whose success is fore-ordained. Particularly when the movement suffers reverses, or when tragedy strikes the individual, fatalistic acceptance

---

[79] *Ibid.*, No. 6, 1963, p. 53; cf. *Znaniye i vera v Boga* (Knowledge and Belief in God), All-Union Society for the Dissemination of Political and Scientific Knowledge, Moscow, 1960, p. 110.

[80] *Op. cit.*, p. 96.

[81] *Ibid.*, p. 31; cf. Malakhova, *op. cit.*, p. 16.

can be remarkably effective in helping them to overcome incipient despair. According to one anti-religious writer, after the war, Baptist preachers

> went to orphaned families, presenting themselves in the role of interpreters of the "will of God," who predestines some to salvation and others to death. They went after the tracks of the unfortunate and grieving as though to "comfort" those who had suffered loss with the idea that before the face of "inscrutable fate" the personal will and action of man means nothing. God, unfathomable in his mercy and in his wrath, predestined each person to his lot even "from the beginning of creation."

> Baptist preachers inculcated a fatalistic outlook on life. In places their preaching had success.[82]

The deterministic element makes fatalistic acceptance possible without necessitating surrender to despair or loss of faith in the ultimate, inevitable success of the movement. The communists, predictably enough, see something profoundly insidious in the Baptist approach to determinism:

> Among the multitudes of sectarian religions, Baptism from the very beginning has distinguished itself by its simple anti-humanism, elevated to the position of a principle. It arises from the dogma of predestination, and on this basis the religion of the Baptists enunciates the primordial sinfulness of man, the absolute powerlessness and uselessness of man in the development of his intellectual and moral powers. "By the perversity of satan" we read in the religious doctrine of the Baptists, "man sinned, fell from God and was deprived of the image of his creator and immediately fell body and soul into the situation of death..."

> ..."Man is a false being" said the Baptist Sukharev (born 1884), in the village of Ranino, in conversation with us, "there is not one man who has not sinned. Well, if Jesus Christ calls us, forgives us, so that the Lord changes us, that is his affair." Man not only is a false being, in the words of the Michurin Baptists, but he is also an insignificant, weak being. "He was created by God's will and what he does is by God's will."[83]

If determinism can be useful in some respects, it can also create grave difficulties arising from the need to find a place within the system for human initiative and action. The Baptists attempt to escape this dilemma with an appeal (which seems logically contradictory) to freedom of the will. The Russian Baptists have never displayed much tendency toward the scholastic consistency of the extreme Calvinists of the West.[84] They find practical resolution of the dilemma in the distinction between the issue of salvation and damnation, which is unconditional, and rewards for the believers, which depend on his conduct.[85]

The Baptists have an apocalyptic tendency in their approach to life. Baptists anticipate the cataclysmic consummation of history, which, marking the downfall of the reign of sin, will usher in the Kingdom of God.

---

[82] *Sovremennoye sektantstvo, op. cit.*, p. 97.

[83] *Ibid.*, pp. 128—129.

[84] E. g., *BV*, No. 4, 1964, pp. 29—30, 35—36.

[85] *Ibid.*, p. 38.

The Baptists in the Ukraine were originally called "Stundists." In what is probably one of history's least likely explanations, one communist author contends, "*Stunde* in German means 'hour'; the Stundists await the hour of rising to the heavenly kingdom."[86] Baptist sermons do, however, have recourse fairly frequently to apocalypticism:

> Quickly, quickly Christ approaches. And then it will already be too late. That will be not only a day of greatest blessing for believers, but also a day of terrible judgement for unbelievers. There will be none in between. Bad it will go for those who do not believe in the crucifixion of Christ..."[87]

This apocalyptic orientation has been on the increase in recent years, perhaps in response to the increasing pressure the Baptists find themselves under.

> A. I. Klibanov said that a new factor, common to all the sects, is a quickening of the interest in eschatological subjects. This is one of the manifestations of the deep gulf between sectarian religious doctrine and life, its inability to find a common ground with the people. Hence, too, the recourse to intimidating people with the "second coming."[88]

The Baptists are strongly messianic in outlook. Their messianism, however, concentrates on the attempt to proselytize among the Russian people and they devote great energy to attracting new converts.[89]

> The use of choral singing along with services has the purpose of creating a special state of reverence among the faithful. The hymns very often employ the motifs of popular Soviet and folk songs, and are not lacking in poetry.
>
> In striving to attract the young, taking advantage of the weakness of our cultural work in some districts, the members of these denominations establish choral and musical groups and arrange social evenings in connection with family celebrations, at which sermons on religious morality are read. The denominations also have celebrated Soviet holidays, such as with picnics on May Day....Members of these sects place particular emphasis on individual work with the faithful. The subject of the individual work is usually someone who has suffered failure in life. Charity is extended to such an individual and attempts made to affect his consciousness and draw him into the congregation.[90]

One of the most striking aspects of the Baptist movement is in its highly energetic approach to life. It seeks total commitment to the cause, requiring, ideally, that the adherent devote all his time, talent and ambition to it, to the exclusion of all else. As an illustration of this trait among the Baptists:

> In scientific-atheistic literature there is a generally accepted opinion that among the sectarians there are direct prohibitions against visiting theatres and cinemas, against listening to the radio, reading newspapers and books, etc.

---

[86] Voronovich, *op. cit.*, p. 5.

[87] *Sovremennoye sektantstvo, op. cit.*, p. 99.

[88] Malakhova, *op. cit.*, p. 16.

[89] *Religion in the USSR, op. cit.*, p. 199.

[90] Muravev and Dmitriev, *op. cit.*, pp. 53—54.

Our research shows that it is not so much direct prohibition as the religious world view which hinders taking an interest in books, theatre and cinemas.[91]

The energetic, totally committed way of the Baptists is visible in their strict adherence to morality and industriousness.[92] According to Charles Foltz: "Nearly everyone I talked with about the churches—including bitterly anti-religious Russians—seemed to agree that the Baptists were sober, hard-working people."[93] The morally clean lives of the Baptists might be expected to exert a powerful appeal among people who have become disillusioned with more jaded or hypo-critical segments of Soviet society.

Throughout the Soviet period the Baptist movement has had a profound degree of social consciousness. Their early reaction to the communist govern-ment was identification with its social programme[94] and Baptists have long emphasized the proletarian origins of Jesus Christ.[95] They elevate good citizen-ship into a virtue, even in times of difficulty,

> in conformity with the teaching of the Bible, which says: "And seek the peace of the city whither I have caused you to be carried away captives, and pray unto the Lord for it: for in the peace thereof shall you have peace." (Jeremiah 29 : 7)[96]

Baptists hold that "God not only founded, but he also preserves the Soviet state"[97] and are not loathe to take responsible roles in the life of the community when permitted.[98] Baptists apparently are able to adapt to a scientifically oriented society,[99] and, according to one Baptist: "Were all like the Baptists, communism would already be built."[100]

Finally, despite the centrifugal tendencies inherent in the movement, the Russian Baptists are a moderately well disciplined organization. New members of a local church are given a period of trial and special help, often under the guidance of two of the more experienced members.[101] When a member leaves for another city, whenever possible the church at his destination is notified in ad-vance.[102] Among pastors in a given area advice and counsel is exchanged.[103]

---

[91] *Sovremennoye sektantstvo, op. cit.*, p. 138.

[92] *Kommunist vooruzhennykh sil* (Communist of the Armed Forces), No. 18, 1964.

[93] Foltz, *op. cit.*, p. 57.

[94] *Sovremennoye sektantstvo, op. cit.*, p. 28.

[95] *Znaniye i vera v Boga, op. cit.*, p. 114; I. D. Pantskhav, ed., *O nekotorykh osobennostyakh sovremennoy religioznoy ideologii* (Some Peculiarities of Contemporary Religious Ideology), Moscow: Moscow University Press, 1964, p. 285.

[96] Alexander Karev, "The Protestant Church in the USSR," *USSR*, No. 6, June, 1963, p. 41.

[97] *Znaniye i vera v Boga, op. cit.*, p. 114.

[98] S. P. Pavlov, "Rely on the Forces of the Public," *Komsomolskaya pravda*, October 27, 1960. Condensed translation in *CDSP*, November 30, 1960, p. 28.

[99] M. I. Shakhnovich, "Vestiges of Religious Mysticism and How to Remove Them," *Voprosy Filosofii*, No. 2, February, 1964. Translation in *RCDA*, May 31, 1964, p. 79.

[100] *Znaniye i vera v Boga, loc. cit.*

[101] *Religion in the USSR, op. cit.*, pp. 135–136; S. Krainov, "Baptists in Russia," *Commonweal*, New York, No. 73, December 30, 1960, p. 360.

[102] *Ibid.*

[103] Voronovich, *op. cit.*, p. 118.

It should be obvious that, at least in terms of this brief catalogue of Baptist characteristics, the segment of society most likely to be attracted to the movement is not the Russian Orthodox, but people of the sort who would be attracted to the Communist Party itself. The Party shares all of these characteristics with the Baptists.

Communism is rationally oriented, with a world view whose outline is relatively easy to grasp (and which, like Baptist doctrine, is also plagued with logical inconsistencies in some points). Communism is dogmatic, looking to the inspired writings of Marx and Engels and Lenin as its Scripture. Mechanistic determinism allows the communist to rely semi-fatalistically on the march of history, and involves him in difficulties in allowing for the actor's ability to influence the course of history. Communism is apocalyptic, looking forward to the communist Utopia being ushered in by the cataclysmic world revolution. The Communist Party seeks to be energetic, demanding total commitment (ideally to the exclusion of all else) of its members. Its messianism differs somewhat from that of the Baptists, giving chief importance to international messianism, although the Party, too, is interested in proselytization, striving to "educate the political consciousness" of the masses of Russia. The social concern of the Baptists is a reflection of communism's deep interest in social betterment, and Baptist discipline harkens back to the disciplinary thrust of the salad days of the Party.

In all of these aspects, then, it would appear that the same sort of person would be attracted either to the Party or to the Baptists; both, it would seem, would draw upon the same psychological type, the element in society which would be most attracted by these characteristics.

Under present circumstances, the Baptists enjoy a few advantages over the Communist Party. The Baptists, because they are all but excluded from the power structure of society, have the aura of a semi-clandestine, persecuted movement,[104] an advantage which the communists have not had since their accession to power, but which may have contributed mightily to their early ability to attract adherents. Furthermore, because they are social outcasts, Baptists may be better able and, more important, highly motivated, to reach out to other individuals on the fringes of society, working with those whom the Party cannot or does not care to reach:

> They well know whom to select as the object of religious work. They went to widowed women, to invalids, to lonely people, to those who they thought either from old age, or for one or another concrete reason, seemed at the given moment outside the unbreakable, active bonds with the working collective of Soviet people. Hoping for success with their preaching they also had contacts with the lower strata of cultural development and actively conducted [their preaching] among the semiliterate.[105]

---

[104] Cf. Peter Deyneka, comp., *The Life and Sufferings of Christians in Solovki and Siberia*, Grand Rapids, Mich.: Zondervan, (no date: ca. 1940), p. 5; I. S. Prokhanoff, *In the Cauldron of Russia*, New York: All-Russian Evangelical Christian Union, 1933, p. 248.

[105] *Sovremennoye sektantstvo, op. cit.*, p. 97.

Under present circumstances of course, these minor advantages held by the Baptists are more than outweighed by the advantage of power held by the Communist Party. However attractive the Baptist movement may be, the fact remains that it is the Party which holds the key to advancement in current Soviet society, and one joins the Baptists only when one is willing to renounce any hope for education, responsibility, prominence or active participation of any significance at all in society. Although anti-religious authors point to the social composition of the movement as evidence of its decadence, it is probably chiefly due to the power structure of society and state limitations that the ranks of the Baptists are composed primarily of the old, the unskilled or semi-skilled, and the poorly educated.[106]

But the fact remains that, theological and ideological considerations aside, the dynamics of the Baptist movement parallel the dynamics of the Party, and the Baptists thus represent a potential competitor to communism. The appeal of the Baptists is by no means limited to the social castaways:[107] the state's anti-religious writers are fully aware of the movement's ability to influence the educated younger generation.[108] The Party seems able to keep this threat in check by means of limiting Baptist activity, but it has not succeeded completely in imposing more severe limitations on them during the current campaign.

A certain caveat, however, is in order in assessing the potential of the Baptists to influence society. In a modern technological society, it is doubtful whether more than a minority of the citizens would find themselves attracted by the characteristics outlined above. Even given absolute freedom, it would not seem likely that the Baptist movement could hope to embrace more than a small minority of the population. This is not, however, to diminish the importance of the influence the movement could have on society. The Communist Party, after all, with all its virtually unlimited freedom in Soviet society, has never succeeded in including more than a tiny fraction of the population in its ranks. But its influence, needless to say, has been out of all proportion to its size.

Considering both the present strength of the Baptists and their potential to compete with the Party, the conclusion would seem to be that the significance of the movement will only increase in the more pluralistic society, which, hopefully, is emerging in the USSR. Should the evolving Communist Party broaden its appeal by discarding some of its more zealous aspects (which, after all, were present in far greater abundance a generation ago) or should the Party disappear entirely, that would not necessarily mean that a vacuum would be left in Soviet society. For the Baptists could then hope to reach the same sort of people which the Party used to reach.

---

[106] *Ibid.*, pp. 23, 95; Muravev and Dmitriev, *op. cit.*, p. 46.

[107] Cf. the treatment of Alyosha in Alexander Solzhenitsyn, *One Day in the Life of Ivan Denisovich*, New York: Praeger, 1963.

[108] Muravev and Dmitriev, *op. cit.*, p. 53.

The Search for New Ideals in the USSR: Some First-Hand Impressions

Peter B. Reddaway

This paper is based on impressions from three visits to the USSR, particularly from my longest and most recent one (September 1963 to May 1964), spent as an exchange scholar at Moscow University. The general atmosphere had changed significantly by 1963 as compared with the period of my first visits in 1960 and 1961. In the interval, serious difficulties had arisen in the economy and cultural life of the Soviet Union and in the world communist movement. Disillusion with Marxism-Leninism, not surprisingly, had therefore deepened.

I have written elsewhere about the fragility and limited extent of Marxist-Leninist belief in the USSR today, and have tried to show that the Soviet leaders themselves often make similar estimates of the situation.[1] The complementary theme of this paper is the current unofficial searching for new, different, more viable ideals. The lack of any reliable quantitative data on this subject—an elusive one even in the most open societies—inevitably makes my observations highly subjective. Nonetheless, the schematic and provisional sketch which follows could without difficulty be illustrated much more widely than is done here, both from literary sources and from personal experiences (although discretion would impose obvious limits on the recounting of these in print).

While the search for new ideals has undoubtedly intensified over the last few years, it is questionable whether it has grown in direct relation to the decline in Marxist-Leninist conviction. For the latter process tends to lead people first into a situation where their deep *emotional* antipathy towards the all-pervasive ideology can find no intellectual support. They have no coherent understanding as to *why* the ideology is false, let alone any knowledge of any truer ideals. As Milosz has written:

> They not only dare not speak, they do not know *what* to say. Logically, everything is as it should be. From the philosophical premises to the collectivization of the farms, everything makes up a single closed whole, a solid and imposing pyramid. The lone individual inevitably asks himself if his antagonism is not wrong; all he can oppose to the entire propaganda apparatus are simply his irrational desires. Should he not, in fact, be ashamed of them?[2]

In figurative terms, he suffers from toothache but does not even know which tooth is aching. Milosz continues: "The Party is vigilantly on guard lest these longings be transmuted into new and vital intellectual formulas adapted to new

---

[1] See "Aspects of Ideological Belief in the Soviet Union," *Soviet Studies*, Glasgow, Vol. XVII, No. 4, April 1966, pp. 473–483.

[2] C. Milosz: *The Captive Mind* (Mercury Books, 1962), pp. 212–213.

conditions and therefore capable of winning over the masses."[3] If, in other words, the Party cannot make people into convinced communists, it at least does its utmost to keep them in a state of "internal emigration" where they are isolated in their uncertainty as to whether any truer alternative values exist, and, if so, which.

Thus there are daunting psychological as well as political barriers to overcome in a quest for new ideals under a communist regime. Indeed, the difficulties facing, for example, a lapsed Catholic in Italy would seem very minor by comparison: a wide range of fully legal religious and political alternatives is available to succour him. Despite the barriers, however, the search for new ideals in the USSR is probably more widespread now than at any time since the years before the revolution. This is not very surprising: as the Stalin years of terror recede, Russians have increasingly been able to take stock of their position. In my experience many of them have come to feel, however inarticulately at times, that although most of the barbarities committed by the Party belong to the past, the present regime will only doubtfully be able to fulfil their future economic requirements and almost certainly not their cultural and spiritual needs.

It is, indeed, symptomatic that the present ruling class shows no meaningful inclination towards its *own* spiritual renewal—Russian friends pointed out that the much-vaunted "return to Leninist norms" could never mean very much as long as the thousands of helpers of Stalin and Beria remained unpunished and indeed formed an important part of the *apparat*, or as long as people of similar type continued to be promoted from the Komsomol. The Party *apparat* was concerned before all else to preserve its own power: no risk could therefore be run of splitting the Party by a purge of its secret police section or by admitting to fundamental past mistakes; therefore no need for any spiritual renewal could be admitted either.

A greater urge to moral reform is noticeable among the Soviet technocracy: the managers, engineers, scientists, planners. Although mostly Party members, they seem often to be more nationalist than communist, the Party turning a blind eye to this in view of its reliance on them. Many of them feel strongly about the need for greater rationality and less Party interference in the economy, in some cases out of a concern for the poverty of the masses. These people dislike verbiage, try to unearth facts about the economy and to proclaim them. Kosygin is probably to some extent representative of this group, and the economist Dr. Aganbegyan could be said to belong to its radical wing. In the company of westerners such people do not, in my experience, proselytize, but, rather, take the more tolerant attitude of: "Your system's probably all right for you. . ." One such man's view of the Soviet future held that individual freedom was the aim, but, Russians being by nature anarchic, firm Party dictatorship would unfortunately be necessary until the advent of economic plenty. Thus the ideals of at least the radical wing of this group might tentatively be summed up as truthfulness, concern for economic reform and the standard of

---

[3] *Ibid.*, p. 213.

living of the people, and, ultimately, some sort of political freedom. These ideals may not be altogether new, but they seem to have spread with the growth of those functional groups in which they predominate.

*

Let us turn now from the Party *apparat* and the Soviet technocracy to those sections of society where the search for new ideals is more definitely going on and where it can better be studied, i.e. among ordinary people and, above all, among the "creative intelligentsia." This search is conducted with varying degrees of consciousness and on very different, if overlapping, levels. The first level may be defined for convenience as that of a man's personal behaviour, in particular towards other people. The second level, less widely attained, concerns his cultural, philosophic and religious views. And the third level, not necessarily "higher" or "lower" than the second, but even less widely attained because of existing deterrents, relates to his political and economic views. An *intelligent* may tend to proceed through "two" to "three" (even possibly to go through "one" after "two" or "three"), whereas a simple, uneducated man may tend to proceed straight from "one" to "three." Whatever the case, however, the three levels overlap widely and are distinguished here only for convenience of discussion.

The many people throughout society in search, consciously or unconsciously, of new ideals on the level of personal behaviour are particularly concerned to root out certain reflexes: for example, those that can still lead to the denunciation of friends or close relatives to the police. They seek to break down social atomisation and fear between people and to be loving and completely loyal to their friends; to be true to their consciences and to avoid being compromised by the authorities; to accept full responsibility for their actions and hence to adopt a critical, even sceptical, attitude towards information from unproven sources; to gain more freedom for themselves (above all to be left alone when desired) and hence to be tolerant towards the quirks of others. They seek, in fact, to re-establish certain principles of common decency; and they do it in the face of the Party's denunciation of such ideals as undesirable "abstract humanism" rather than the approved "socialist humanism" (this latter, we may note, involves proselytizing foreigners, converting the religious, and cooperating with the "socially prophylactic" secret police).

To illustrate some of the foregoing, it should first be pointed out that themes concerning common decency abound in the "liberal" literature of the post-Stalin years and have been particularly explicit in underground literature. A recent poem[4] from an underground journal ends:

> But wherever my path may lie,
> The superstition of Love and Truth
> shall be the measure of my deeds.

As for individual responsibility, the journal's editorial trusts that if its authors suffer for their participation "the consequences will not be too tragic and you

---

[4] "A Crucible of Sorrows," by Makar Slavkov, *Grani*, No. 59, p. 54.

will not cease to be artists who answer for every little thought and word with everything you have, even your lives."[5] Concerning tolerance, the short-story writer Kazakov and others have shown the way by often depicting people with religious or unorthodox political views as fascinating and even sympathetic characters. It was also noticeable in Moscow University how few students would help the authorities to force people against their will into unpopular extra duties or compulsory lectures. Often the authorities would in fact give up, thus showing some tolerance, and it would be left to the university newspaper to complain, for example, that less than half the physics students were going to the compulsory lectures on scientific communism. Similarly, only a few activists would denounce a student found to be religious, and not many more would be actively anti-semitic. Nevertheless, it was surprising to find that several generally tolerant people became irrational on the subject of anti-semitism. Less surprising, but of great interest, was the almost unanimous support to be found for capital punishment.

The growth of the ideal of loyalty to one's friends could be seen in the spread of unofficial literary and literary-political discussion groups. The very existence of these depended on no member betraying his group in any way to an unreliable outsider. In this connection the trial of Sinyavsky and Daniel interestingly showed how various friends had known of their activity for several years but never given them away. Not surprisingly, in any circumstances where loyalty is essential, the penalty for treachery tends to be severe: a designer at a Moscow theatre, for example, suspected by his fellows of being an informer, had all his private paintings burnt and lost his job.

The more admirable aspects of the search for new ideals in personal behaviour should not be allowed to obscure its less attractive sides. The widespread yearning for freedom, self-expression and an end to hypocrisy often leads, in a society with so few channels for such urges, to various forms of licence (ironically enough, well known in the West). Thus, hooliganism, crime, drug-taking, a love of anarchy, an indulgence in sex and its perversions have become the ideals of an increasing and surprisingly large number of, especially, young people. In a more minor key, it may also be noted that a proportion of the intelligentsia with admirable ideals of personal behaviour towards their friends seem, particularly after achieving a measure of material ease in their own lives, to forget about the unfortunate majority which still lives in poverty. This reluctance to think ideals through to their logical conclusion is, of course, a widespread enough phenomenon in any country.

*

An individual's search for new ideals in cultural, philosophic and religious matters can, as suggested earlier, come before or after (or simultaneously with) his establishment of a code of personal behaviour. The main preoccupations in this sphere in the USSR today seem to be (1) to identify the most valuable components in Russia's past and present by weighing up her whole cultural

[5] Editorial to *Sfinsky*, *ibid.*, p. 10.

heritage and re-establishing contact between the different sections of her contemporary society; (2) to determine the nature of Russia's cultural relation to the outside world, in particular to the West; and (3) on the basis of (1) and (2) and of an examination of the Russian psyche under modern conditions, to construct a new philosophy and culture relevant to Russia's spiritual needs.

An underground poem in tune with the search for Russia's roots proclaims:

> And these are the highest values:
> Patriotism and love of one's neighbor,
> Truth and democracy,
> Poetry and history.
> Love and bread...[6]

The concern with Russia's history appears in many forms. Most notably, her religious past becomes of great importance, and many young people spend their summer vacations walking from old church to old church, collecting and studying icons, and spending the night in peasants' huts. Writers like Soloukhin and Leonov lead public campaigns of protest at the needless destruction or neglect of religious monuments. And peasants and their religous ways are described in the works of Solzhenitsyn, Kazakov, Yashin and others. The feeling is widespread that in the countryside important spiritual and human values have miraculously been preserved through the upheavals of war, revolution and industrialization, and that it is important to regain them for the whole nation.

Similarly, it is felt that bridges must be built to the values of the intelligentsia of the tsarist and pre-Stalinist periods. The memoirs of Chukovsky, Paustovsky and Ehrenburg are read avidly, as are the works of Tsvetaeva, Mandelshtam, Berdyaev, the Symbolists and, in particular perhaps, Dostoevsky, Chekhov and Pasternak. The appeal of Dostoevsky lies above all in his turbulent psychological conflicts and his insight into the grotesque sides of existence; that of Chekhov in the perpetual frustration through both social and psychological causes of his characters' impulses to self-sacrifice; and that of Pasternak in his inspiring integrity in refusing to compromise his noble ideals. Not surprisingly, these appeals strike deeply personal chords in sensitive readers in contemporary Russia.

When trying to reunite the nation and to feel its pulse, the "searching" intelligentsia seems to have the most difficulty in making contact with the proletariat. For the latter has preserved much less from the past than the peasantry. In my experience and that of Russian friends, however, the proletariat is increasingly resolute in asserting its right to human dignity in the face of exploitation. It may also be noted that working-class people are now on occasion described in literature, by writers like Syomin and Aksyonov, with a feeling of conviction.

Assessors of Russia's relation to the outside world conclude almost unanimously that Russia belongs culturally to Europe. This holds true even though she possesses many special features, including the eastern brand of Christianity. A notable difference of emphasis does appear, however, between those like

---

[6] A poem by A. Mikhailov in *ibid.*, p. 48.

Solzhenitsyn or Tvardovsky who tend to rejoice in the special features, and those like Ehrenburg and Yevtushenko who have more cosmopolitan tastes. Nevertheless, almost all "searchers" respect the bulk of western cultural achievements, seek contact with them, and often, for example, listen to western radio stations. Only a small and rather extreme category, consisting of Leonov and certain younger fanatics, believe in the doom of western culture and the moral regeneration of the world through the exclusive agency of Orthodoxy. All "searchers" seem to regard specifically communist culture, in Russia at least, as bankrupt.

One of the most difficult and important tasks for "searchers" has been to start the exploration of the contemporary Russian psyche. As Stalin's ban on introspection has remained to a considerable extent in force, much work still lies ahead. Without this, no new philosophy will ever be able to feel itself securely based. Besides determined efforts to obtain and read the classics of Western psychology and moral science, the search goes on in literature too. Here poets like Blok and Akhmatova, with their descriptions of highly personal emotions, provide the starting point, and such writers as Akhmadulina, Yevtushenko and Bitov have established some continuity. Going further, Voznesensky and a few others have ventured into the fruitful field of surrealism; so too, more decisively, have various underground writers, including the imprisoned Sinyavsky and Daniel. In the field of more directly moral problems, Tendryakov and Okudzhava arouse especial interest by posing difficult questions about death, human tragedy or the nature of patriotism. Underground literature also reclaims the right to be openly pessimistic if desired:

> Here everything reeks of gradual death...
> We are fishermen. Here people don't cry,
> But only drink, and drink, and drink,
> And sing dreadful songs,
> And pay for their songs with their lives.[7]

The overriding concern of many young "searchers" is, in fact, to discover and face up to their own real nature: they can then be true to this in their lives. Some of the dominant strands in the search are therefore existentialist in nature. It is even thought possible that Marxism-Leninism might eventually move in this direction, in an effort to regenerate some appeal.

In the specifically religious sphere, the search tends, in my experience, to concern itself somewhat more with Orthodox *values* than with the presently constituted Orthodox Church. Many regard the latter as in certain respects, especially that of its leadership, unjustifiably compromised. Not only the Bible and Orthodox thinkers, however, are studied, but also the literature of, notably, Judaism and Buddhism. Moreover, among many people of very different stations who have never seen a Bible or attended a church, a growing feeling seems to exist that "Perhaps there is something helpful in religion after all." Certainly, one cannot help sensing in Russia that religious inclinations of widely varying sorts are on the increase, however little they may manifest themselves on the surface.

---

[7] By V. Kovshin, *ibid.*, p. 40.

The most gripping play I saw in Moscow was the second performance of Tend-ryakov's "Without a Cross !" at the Sovremennik Theatre.[8] A genuine tragedy which revolved round an evenly matched struggle between the forces of belief and unbelief, it deliberately left unclear where the author's and producer's own sympathies really lay. The tense absorption of the audience seemed to stem both from the unusually powerful tragedy and, in particular, from their own indentification with the hard problem of whether, and, if so, how to believe.

*

Just as church-going among young people may be much inhibited by the political and psychological deterrents, so too is the search for new political ideals. Indeed, some individuals deliberately distract themselves in every possible way to avoid the psychological burden which they know, consciously or subconsciously, would be incurred by thinking their beliefs through to their logical political conclusions. One safety valve has been developed in the form of the increasingly popular political joke, but this by its nature is more destructive than constructive.

As regards more positive searching, "neo-Leninism" seemed in 1963–64 to have more or less burnt itself out. With political jokes even beginning to touch the hitherto sacrosanct Lenin, the seed of doubt which asked how far Stalinism was inherent in Leninism had evidently begun to put down roots. Neo-Leninism survives, in fact, mainly as a useful tactic. For no one I met believed any longer that the Party could be significantly reformed from within. If it were genuinely to democratize itself, it would dig its own grave. Writers like Bondarev, Solzhenitsyn, Akhmatova, Yevtushenko and Slutsky have all obliquely reflected the widespread public feeling that many people should be brought to account for the Stalinist terror. Not surprisingly, the Party fears the consequences of any such step. Faced with political immobilism of this sort, "searchers" seem increasingly to feel that Stalinism and even communism have been a nightmare episode in Russia's history, whatever advances these may have brought, and that it is essential to build for the future on more traditionally Russian and popular values. The extreme view, in underground literature, speaks of "the chains of October" and of Russians as "the slaves of the free-est constitutions."[9]

The most frequently mentioned requirements for an acceptable future political order are that Russia should be led by worthy men; that the mass of her people should be rid of their poverty; that the state should contain only those non-Russians who genuinely want to belong (Caucasian nationalism, in particular, was in evidence in Moscow University); that agriculture should be basically de-collectivized (a view widely held outside "searcher" circles too); and that legality should be restored, based on an independent judiciary. Views on industry seem to vary greatly.

---

[8] The play was taken off after a few performances and only reinstated later in an altered and less interesting form.

[9] From a poem by E. Golovin, *ibid.*, p. 28.

Many of these visions are doubtless utopian, but for discussion groups and even the few active political groups (usually heard of by outsiders only when caught) they constitute the subjects for debate. Although participation in this debate remains highly risky, and apparently confined to narrow circles, it was believed in Russia in 1964 that the latter were widening.

*

Such a broad survey of the search for new ideals in Russia can only be highly superficial. Nevertheless, gain may perhaps accrue from treating the subject rather comprehensively, if, of course, over-schematically. The danger also arises of mistakenly giving the impression of a more feverish search going on in Russia than is in fact the case: Russia certainly contains at least her share of human weakness, and this is duly compounded by a political system well designed for the systematic corruption of personal integrity. Many Russian friends had full political trust in only one other person, or, in one case, in no one. The scale of the search for new ideals cannot be reliably estimated. Surely, however, it is for the ultimate good of Russia and the world that at least some forces for personal, cultural and political renewal are at work and growing.

The Tenacity of Islam in Soviet Central Asia

Georg von Stackelberg

During the last two decades many conferences and symposiums on Islam have been held in Western Europe and the United States, such as those in Paris (1948), Istanbul (1951), Liège and Spa (1953), Cambridge (1954), Bordeaux (1956) and Munich (1957), to mention only a few. Two of the most interesting meetings were held in New York in 1960 and in Washington in 1962, both organised by the Institute for the Study of the USSR in Munich, in conjunction with the Institute for the Study of the Middle East. The first conference was on "Islam and Communism,"[1] and the second dealt specifically with the Moslem peoples of the Soviet Union. In addition to these discussions on a subject that is attracting more and more attention in the West there have recently appeared a number of valuable studies to which reference may profitably be made (see appended Bibliography).

The Moslem peoples of Central Asia came under Russian rule as a result of the expansionist policy of the Tsarist Empire. This policy was continued by the Soviet leaders, who turned the Russian protectorates of Bukhara (an Emirate) and Khiva (a Khanate), into people's republics in 1919–1920, liquidating them again in 1924 as part of the new policy of "national demarcation of Central Asia." The Soviet Union thus held sway over vast territories containing a population that had adopted the Moslem religion and culture long before it fell under the domination of the Tsars. The Azerbaidzhanis embraced Islam in the seventh century, the Turkestanis in the eighth, the Bulgars in the tenth, the Golden Horde in the thirteenth century and the Adzhars of Southern Georgia in the sixteenth century. Part of the population of Abkhazia became Moslem in the seventeenth and eighteenth centuries. The Ossetians, and the Chechens and Kabardinians of the Northern Caucasus had already been converted by the eighteenth and seventeenth centuries respectively.

The deep roots of the Moslem religion in the territories inherited by the Soviet regime from the Tsarist Empire explain the vitality and resilience of Islam today in these areas, and its ability to adapt itself to the new social and economic conditions. According to approximate estimates based on the 1959 Soviet census, the USSR has a Moslem population of about 25 million, which is about 12 per cent of the total population. It is the fourth largest Moslem group in the world (the total Moslem population of the globe amounts to 400 million). This large body of followers of Islam in the Soviet Union naturally has an effect on Soviet policy towards the Moslem states of Asia and Africa, whom Moscow takes pains not to offend.

The Uzbeks occupy fourth place numerically among the non-Russian nationalities of the Soviet Union and are the most numerous of the Moslem peoples.

---

[1] *Islam and Communism*, ed. by Jaan Pennar, New York, 1960.

There are altogether 6,015,000 Uzbeks, of whom 5,038,000 live in Uzbekistan. Next come the Tatars (4,970,000), Kazakhs (3,622,000), Azerbaidzhanis (2,940,000), Tadzhiks (1,397,000), Turkmen (1,000,000), Bashkirs (989,000) and the Kirghiz (969,000). According to the 1959 census, the total number of Moslem peoples living in the North Caucasus amounted to about 2 million, including the peoples of Daghestan (Nogai, Kumyks, Avars, Lezghins, Laks, etc., totalling 945,000), the Chechens (418,000), Ingush (106,000), Kabardinians (204,000), Cherkess (30,000), Adighei (80,000), Karachai (81,000), Balkars (42,000) and Ossetians, who number 413,000, one-third being Moslems. Neither the 1939 nor the 1959 census gives figures for the Crimean Tatars, who were all deported in 1946 and have not as yet returned to their homeland. According to the 1926 census, there were 180,000 of them in the Soviet Union. There are other smaller Moslem minorities also. These include the Uighurs (95,000), Kurds (59,000, including the Ezid Kurds), the Dungani (22,000), Iranians (20,000), Abazins (19,600), Arabs (8,000), Beludzhi (7,800), Albanians (5,000), Afghans (1,900), Georgian Adzhars and Abkhazians (74,000).

Soviet statistics give no clue to the number of Moslems who actually remain believers and those who have abandoned their religion. TASS has reported the Soviet Mufti, Ziya-ud-din Babakhanov, who headed the Soviet Moslem delegation at the 1965 Afro-Asian conference in Bandung, as stating in his address that he represented twenty million Moslems in the Soviet Union, which means that the head of the "Spiritual Directorate of the Moslems of Central Asia and Kazakhstan" has overlooked five million of the faithful if the census figures above are correct.

Towards the end of the pre-Revolutionary period an attempt to shake off medieval scholasticism and to adapt religious educational principles to the technical achievements of European civilization became observable among the Moslem intelligentsia in various parts of the Russian Empire, particularly in the Volga Region, the Crimea, Turkestan and Azerbaidzhan. These Moslem reformers, who were known as *jadidists*, urged that children be taught to read and write according to modern teaching methods and that, in addition to religious subjects, science should be placed on the curriculum. As a result of this agitation, modern schools were set up at the end of the nineteenth and in the early twentieth centuries in Kazan, Bakhchisarai, Samarkand, Tashkent, and certain other towns in Turkestan.

The reformist ideas expounded by the Moslem *djadid* movement were closely bound up with the idea of cultural unification of all the Turkic peoples, and in the early 1900's a demand for wider political rights for all Russian Moslems was advanced, followed in 1917 by a further demand for the right to self-determination or complete independence to be granted to territories containing the bulk of the Moslem population of the defunct Russian Empire. After the Revolution Russian Moslems became a political force, as was evidenced by the decisions and resolutions of the First All-Moslem Congress held in Moscow in 1917, the Second

Congress of Moslem Clergy in Ufa in July of the same year, and at other conventions elsewhere. Under this pressure the Soviet communist leaders were forced during the first few years after the Revolution to treat Islam not only as a religion but also as a potent political movement representing millions of Moslems. This explains the conciliatory policy adopted by Moscow and reflected in the famous declaration of November 20, 1917, made by the Soviet government to all Moslem workers, in which the latter were promised religious freedom and inviolability of their customs and national and cultural traditions. Another concession was the decree passed by the Council of People's Commissars on December 9, 1917, ordering the State Library in Petrograd to hand over the holy Koran of Osman to the Moslem Regional Congress, then in session. This Koran had been looted from Samarkand by the Russians after their conquest of the Emirate. On July 14, 1918, there followed an appeal from Moscow to all Moslem workers to join the Moslem "socialist army;" in 1919 permission was granted to set up a "Council of Moslem Clergy" for Turkestan; in 1922 confiscated property belonging to the Moslem clergy, was restored, *shariat* courts of law once again permitted, and Friday recognised as the Moslem day of rest.

Stalin's speech at the Congress of the Peoples of Daghestan on November 13, 1920, in Temir-Khan-Shur, in which he declared that "Daghestan must be governed in accordance with its national peculiarities and customs," and that "the Soviet government considers the *shariat* to be as rightful and customary a law as any in force among other peoples of the USSR,"[2] was calculated to win the sympathies of the Moslems and set the keynote for the policy pursued by the Soviet government during this period. But the change of attitude was not long in coming: in his speech on April 21, 1921, at the Constituent Assembly of the Gorskaya ASSR in the North Caucasus, the Soviet leader, Kirov, cast doubt on the legitimacy of the *shariat* by saying: "If old laws and precepts are revived in your courts, then such courts should be closed and sealed despite all our respect for the *shariat*."[3]

Once its control over the Moslem territories was secured, the Soviet government ceased to bother to conciliate the inhabitants and launched a campaign designed openly to undermine Islam. Church property was confiscated, many mosques, theological schools (*makhtab*) and Moslem colleges (*medresseh*) closed, mullahs arrested and deported (especially during the Yezhov purges of 1936–38) and *shariat* courts abolished. Finally, Friday was declared to be no longer a Moslem holiday. These measures weakened the influence of the mullahs and prevented the young generation from being brought up in the spirit of Islam by placing a ban on the observances imposed on Moslems by their canon law.

During the Second World War the Soviet government reversed its policy of persecuting religion in order to bolster the national morale, and Islam benefited from this new attitude. The Moslem faith became "legal" once again, and in

[2] I. V. Stalin, *Sochineniya* (Works), Moscow, Vol. IV, 1957, pp. 395–396.

[3] S. M. Kirov, *Izbranniye stati i rechi 1912–1934* (Selected Articles and Speeches, 1912–1934), Moscow, 1937, pp. 77–83.

1941 four state-approved administrative bodies, known as "Spiritual Directorates," were set up. These directorates were responsible for, respectively, the Moslems of Central Asia and Kazakhstan (headquarters in Tashkent), those living in the European part of the USSR (headquarters in Ufa), those in the North Caucasus and Daghestan (headquarters in Buinaksk) and those in the Transcaucasus (headquarters in Baku). The Council for Religious Cult Affairs, established in 1944, acted as intermediary between these organizations and the Soviet government.

This innovation was accompanied by further relaxation of the official policy towards Islam after the end of the war, partly as a consequence of Soviet efforts to establish friendly relations with the Moslem countries of Afro-Asia. This policy of granting recognition to the Moslem religion led to the formation of an "approved" clergy, i.e. mullahs appointed by the Spiritual Directorates, and to the appearance of "illegal" mullahs who are chosen by their communities without reference to the Directorates, which were regarded as being subordinate to the regime. Absence of persecution of Islam does not, however, mean that the latter enjoys full liberty in the Soviet Union. Restrictions on ecclesiastical organization exist and dissemination of anti-religious propaganda remains the order of the day. Nevertheless, the Soviet government does its best to convince Moslem opinion abroad that adherents of Islam within its borders enjoy complete freedom of belief. To this end, demonstrative measures are taken for foreign consumption. Groups of Soviet Moslems are permitted to make the pilgrimage to Mecca, and when prominent personages from Moslem countries pay state visits they are invited to attend religious services celebrated with much pomp. Members of the Soviet Moslem "Spiritual Directorates" give interviews to visiting delegations from Islamic countries in which they paint a rosy picture of religious life in the Soviet Union, and more often than not "legal mullahs" are used to propagate Soviet foreign policy aims: for example, the spiritual head of the Moslems in European Russia and Siberia, Mufti Khiyalitdinov, delivered a speech on the need for disarmament and peace at the All-Union Conference of Moslem Clergy held in Tashkent in 1962. As the Soviet press reported at the time:

> Participants in the conference stressed the provocative nature of slander concerning the life of Moslems in the USSR, circulated by imperialist propaganda in order to bring about a split within the international Moslem movement for universal peace and friendship among nations.[4]

The conference also sent a letter of thanks to Khrushchev "for the courage and restraint that he displayed over the Cuban crisis." However, success does not always attend efforts to persuade the Moslem countries outside the Soviet Union of the latter's indulgence towards Islam. The resolutions adopted by the second session of the Islamic Congress in Mecca (April 17 to 24, 1966) expressed concern over the "deplorable" position of Moslems residing in the Soviet Union and China, and condemned the "imperialist" drive to destroy the national identity of

---

[4] *Pravda vostoka*, November 1, 1962.

millions of Soviet and Chinese Moslems by discriminating against their religion, mother tongue and heritage.

In the Soviet Union the principal weapon in use at the present time to sap the influence of Islam is atheist propaganda, comprising lectures, pamphlets and books, establishment of anti-religious museums, the distribution of anti-religious posters ridiculing Moslem rituals, and public criticism of those who observe them, etc. This propaganda campaign is not new: around 1925, Soviet newspapers and periodicals began criticizing Islam in the languages of the various Moslem peoples. Among such publications were the monthly Tatar and Uzbek periodical *Allakhsyzlar* (The Godless), the Tatar newspaper *Dinsezlar* (The Atheists), published in Kazan, the monthly anti-religious journal *Fen khem din* (Science and Religion), and others. The state publishing house *Ateist* published in 1931 a compendium of anti-Islamic works, as well as numerous pamphlets, books and articles refuting Islam as a religion. Upon the outbreak of war in 1941, publication of atheist propaganda was discontinued, only to be revived in 1947 when the Association of Militant Godless was dissolved and the Society for Dissemination of Political and Scientific Knowledge established, which in turn was renamed the All-Union *Znaniye* (Knowledge) Society. The Society's function is to publish anti-religious literature, including anti-Islamic, establish "atheist corners" in clubs, and organize permanent and mobile anti-religious exhibitions. The "Atheist Universities" at Ufa and Ashkhabad were also founded by the Society at the end of the 1950's.

The most noteworthy anti-Islamic books are those by L. I. Klimovich, published by the USSR Academy of Sciences, and containing a mixture of objective fact and cheap anti-religious propaganda.[5] In a drive to develop more effective ways of combatting Islam, special republican and oblast meetings have been held in the Soviet Union, such as the "All-Russian Theoretical Conference on Problems Relating to the Remnants of Islam," convened in late 1960 at Makhachkala, the capital of Daghestan, and the Ideological Conference held in 1964 in Dushanbe, capital of Tadzhikistan, attended by delegates from a number of other republics and devoted to measures for co-ordinating the anti-religious propaganda campaign against Islam.

Analysis of Soviet newspapers and periodicals show, however, that despite the growing intensity of this campaign, Islam continues to command a strong following, even among the young generation, including Party and Komsomol members. It even seems that the number of practicing believers has increased rather than decreased over the last few years. It is reported from Kazakhstan that a religious service at a mosque in the Chimkent Oblast was attended by 4,000 faithful, of whom "every tenth participant was a Komsomol member."[6] And a Kirghiz newspaper complains that "religious survivals continue to persist among certain sections of our young people."[7] An oblast Party committee secre-

---

[5] L. I. Klimovich, *Islam*, 2nd ed., Moscow, 1965.

[6] *Leninskaya smena*, February 14, 1965.

[7] *Komsomolets Kirghizii*, April 25, 1965.

tary in Turkmenia made a statement to the press in which he declared that "certain elements among the population still fall prey to religious prejudice and superstitions," and that "even young people—young lads and girls brought up in our times and at Soviet schools—may be seen among the visitors to the 'holy places' of Ovezdzhan-Khodzha, Aotan-Baba, and many others."[8] D. R. Rasulov, First Party Secretary of Tadzhikistan, said at a plenary session of the Central Committee of the republic that the Moslem clergy's influence on the young generation had started to produce harmful effects, and that the mullahs in the republic had succeeded in establishing schools for teaching the religious dogmas of Islam to children in Leninabad, Kurgan-Tyube and Kolkhozobad.[9] Another Party meeting in Tadzhikistan heard delegates say that even teachers were observing religious rites,[10] while from Moscow itself it is reported that on Moslem holy days young Tatars working in the capital regularly attend the mosque.[11]

Dozens of similar examples showing that Islam has a hold over young Moslems may be found in both Soviet newspapers and periodicals. Apparently numerous Party members in the Moslem areas of the country also observe the rites of their faith. The First Party Secretary of Azerbaidzhan, Akhundov, told a plenary Central Committee meeting that "in some towns and regions even communists, Komsomol members and teachers have been seen attending the *mageram* service.[12] And the press has complained that a member of the Baku raion Party committee observes religious rites.[13] The same story comes from Uzbekistan, where the First Party Secretary, Rashidov, publicly condemned observance of religious rites on the part of Party members, saying: "At his house the secretary of the Party organisation on the "Leningrad" collective farm in the Babkent raion of Bukhara Oblast staged in January of this year a religious ceremony called *khatim-koran*[14] attended by about a hundred persons. Other Party members were also present."[15] It has also been reported that "many believers congregate at the places of Moslem pilgrimage, known as *mazar*, at the shrines of Kuk-Temir-ata and Sultan Sandzhar, and that the moving spirit behind these displays of piety is the manager of the "N. S. Khrushchev" collective farm, Party member Navruz Khaidarov, who lives in the vicinity of the holy shrines and who "has helped to erect a sturdy palisade round the *mazar* and to put it in order."[16]

A striking case of uninhibited observance of ancient Moslem customs in Soviet Central Asia comes from Kirghizia, where Kamal Tursunbaev, manager of the Gulchinskaya electric power station, organised an elaborate funeral feast

---

[8] *Turkmenskaya iskra*, February 18, 1962.

[9] *Kommunist Tadzhikistana*, June 10, 1963.

[10] *Ibid.*, January 7, 1963.

[11] *Moskovsky komsomolets*, October 29, 1964.

[12] *Bakinsky rabochy*, July 4, 1963.

[13] *Ibid.*, September 9, 1962.

[14] Cover-to-cover perusal of the Koran on the death of a relative, immediately after the funeral and on the seventh and fortieth day after his death.

[15] *Pravda vostoka*, July 13, 1963.

[16] *Ibid.*, September 26, 1962.

when his father died, and invited a large concourse of local people, in whose honour he slaughtered a considerable number of farm animals, including eighty sheep.[17]

All the indications are that Islam is more than holding its own in the face of official hostility. The Central Asian press reports that "whereas three to five years ago no more than thirty-odd elderly people were to be seen frequenting mosques, there are now thousands of worshippers."[18] And there is a flourishing, but illegal, theological college in Tadzhikistan, so it is reported.[19] According to Party Secretary Akhundov, "active work carried out by the clergy—illegal mullahs—has been observable in many regions of Azerbaidzhan, and mosques have been reopened without permission."[20] "Judging by incomplete data, approximately 100 mosques and many holy shrines have been opened in the last two years in the mountain and alpine regions of Tadzhikistan alone."[21]

Recurrent articles and press reports indicate that the number of Moslem worshippers attending mosques has been growing steadily over wide areas, and not only in the Moslem regions of the Soviet Union: "no less than 12,000 Moslem believers gather at the mosque of Leningrad on religious holidays," it is stated,[22] and "on big Moslem feast-days, the adjacent alleys, gateways, and courtyards surrounding the mosque in Moscow are crammed with the faithful."[23] And not only in the places of worship: "there are two places in Moscow where the followers of Mohammed meet—the Izmailov People's Recreation Park, in addition to the mosque."[24]

Favourite shrines attracting considerable numbers of Moslem pilgrims include Mount Suleiman in Kirghizia. Here the visitors are not deterred by the fact that Komsomol guards have been posted all round the mountain to keep them away. When the urban Party committee decided to pull down the shrine on the hill, the Moslem labourers who were sent to do the job refused.[25] *Ramadan*, the great Moslem fast, is also religiously observed in the Soviet Union, notwithstanding particularly intensive efforts to abolish it on the part of the authorities; babies are invariably circumcised, as tradition requires, and marriages are celebrated according to the age-old customs. Nor is the mullah absent when a funeral takes place. The Daghestan newspaper *Leninskoye znamya*, published in Makhachkala, complains about "survivals of the past" being difficult to eradicate among Moslem women, and refers especially to marriage ceremonies performed in accordance with the *shariat*. The newspaper cites cases of young couples who, after having

---

17 *Ala Too*, No. 7, 1965, p. 105.
18 *Leninskaya smena*, February 14, 1965.
19 *Komsomolskaya pravda*, October 6, 1964.
20 *Bakinsky rabochy*, June 5, 1963.
21 *Pravda*, May 27, 1963.
22 *Leningradskaya pravda*, June 19, 1965.
23 *Moskovsky komsomolets*, October 29, 1964.
24 *Vechernyaya Moskva*, August 29, 1964.
25 *Komsomolets Kirghizii*, March 1, 1964.

married in a registry office, as Soviet law requires, go to their mullah for the religious ceremony.

An interesting new development that shows the aggressive resilience of Islam is revealed in the disclosure by the press that the clergy serving the mosques are now producing their own religious literature in defiance of the ban on such publications. Apparently there is no shortage of money for this purpose: one Soviet paper writes that thanks to "the abundant means at the disposal of the mosques, distribution of photocopies of religious texts has been organized,"[26] and "at a mosque in Moscow, the mullahs disseminate translations of the Koran."[27]

As a result of changed economic and social conditions in the Soviet Moslem republics, the inhabitants are not able to observe many of the *shariat* laws. Moslem peasants working on collective and state farms are not allowed to stop work in order to perform their daily religious rites, consisting of five prayer intervals, nor are office employees allowed to do this. It is noteworthy, however, that despite the abolition of the *zekat* or ecclesiastical tax imposed on the faithful, the Moslem clergy appears to be receiving ample contributions from the faithful in order to carry on its activities. Major impediments still, of course, stand in the way of Islamic culture and Koranic tradition, since very few theological colleges survive, and the Cyrillic alphabet, which replaced the Arabic script in the 1930's, has effectively cut off the young generation from Islamic literature. The pilgrimage to Mecca and Medina (the *hadj*) may only be made by small groups of Soviet Moslems, and whenever such groups return, TASS exploits the occasion for publicity purposes. The number of pilgrims is never stated, but it is estimated that they vary between twenty and forty persons.

The above shows that Soviet atheist propaganda has not had the desired effect on the Moslem population, which has tended to react with indifference: the ancient, deeply-ingrained obedience to the Koran and its precepts is still very much in evidence, although not all practicing Moslems are necessarily genuinely convinced; many observe the rites in order not to become outsiders in a Moslem milieu. The scant impact of atheist propaganda, even very often among young Moslems, is revealed by such press reports as one entitled "In our Region it is Difficult to be an Atheist," in which a certain Baidulaev complains about "lectures being primarily attended by atheists. Those who believe in God do not turn up."[28] So apparently there is much preaching to the converted, and the press has sounded the alarm to the effect that Islam cannot be expected to disappear of its own, any more than other religions, and in order to accelerate its eradication, an urgent call is made for attack on a unified front, with every Komsomol member called upon to become a militant atheist.[29] Yet, the reports delivered by the First Party Secretaries of Azerbaidzhan, Uzbekistan, and Turkmenia at their respective Party congresses, from which quotations have been given above, are vivid proof

---

[26] *Leninskaya smena*, April 14, 1965.

[27] *Moskovsky komsomolets*, October 29, 1964.

[28] *Pravda vostoka*, November 26, 1962.

[29] *Komsomolskaya pravda*, February 25, 1964.

of the negative results of anti-Islamic propaganda. Akhundov (Azerbaidzhan) declared: "It is necessary to deal regularly with problems relating to scientific atheist propaganda and to ensure its purposefulness and efficacy." He went on to say that the Azerbaidzhani Party Central Committee had already worked out and implemented measures for combatting religion in the Republic, such as publication of a number of books and pamphlets on scientific atheism, and organization of conferences, debates and discussion evenings. He admitted, nevertheless, that "in many localities scientific atheist propaganda is still being conducted half-heartedly."[30] Rashidov (Uzbekistan) disclosed that "religious survivals are still alive" and that a constant struggle had to be waged against them. Despite the fact that the Party has for many years combatted Islam, the latter "still continues to exert an influence on the Moslems of Uzbekistan." In order to liquidate these "survivals," a "public scientific and methodological council" has been created in Uzbekistan, the members of whom include noted specialists, teachers at higher educational establishments, Party members, and representatives of soviet and other public organizations, whose duty it will be to coordinate anti-religious work throughout the Republic.[31] The First Party Secretary of Turkmenia, B. Ovezov, also complained about "the flourishing illegal activities of mullahs in a number of localities," and about Party committees in many regions that confine themselves to "merely taking cognizance of these cases, and fail to take active, systematic and well thought-out counter-measures."[32] These remarks suggest that the local Party organizations have virtually given up trying to inculcate atheist propaganda into the Moslem population.

In the light of the above one may ask two questions: (1) What causes the Soviet leaders to persist in their efforts to discredit Islam as a religion? and (2) how does one account for the tenacious way in which Soviet Moslems are clinging to their faith, traditions and customs? In answer to (1) the Soviet press declares that survivals of religion hamper the building of a communist society. In the Soviet foreword to the Russian translation of Henri Masset's book *L'Islam*, it is stated:

> The follower of any religious teaching (including Moslems) not only wastes his time on religious rites but also assumes that the real life in this world is nothing but a preparation for life after death. Therefore, the believer is in no position to devote himself unreservedly to labour in the name of the further development of the advanced society in which he lives. Religious holidays divert his mind from creative labour, and both sacrifices and contributions to the benefit of the clergy inflict material harm on the workers.[33]

Among the time- and money-consuming practices mentioned in this foreword are the visits to holy places (*mazar*) and other forms of pilgrimage. The most pressing reason, however, behind the persistent antireligious propaganda campaign is the effort to dissolve the sense of national identity of the Moslem peoples

---

[30] *Bakinsky rabochy*, February 25, 1966.

[31] *Pravda vostoka*, March 4, 1966.

[32] *Turkmenskaya iskra*, February 25, 1966.

[33] A. Masset, *Islam*, Moscow, 1963; see preface by Ye. A. Belyaeva, p. 4.

of the Soviet Union by means of gradual Russification and settlement of non-Moslems on Moslem territories, etc. The Moslem faith is rooted in age-old tradition and therefore represents an obstacle to this policy aimed at creating one single "Soviet" culture and way of life in which national differences disappear. Moslems regard Islam not only as the revelation of Allah through the Prophet, but also as an organic part of their national consciousness and culture. The following incident, recounted in the Kirghiz press, provides an example of this attitude: a candidate of historical sciences and lecturer in the department of philosophy at the University was giving an antireligious lecture on a Kirghiz collective farm. He himself was a Kirghiz and a young farm labourer asked him whether he was a Moslem. The lecturer replied that he was not a Moslem but an atheist, a "godless man who does not believe in any religion or god." After having impatiently listened to him, the young labourer exclaimed: "How dare you call yourself an atheist! Being a Kirghiz makes you a Moslem!" In other words, membership of a certain nationality means automatically that a man must worship Islam.[34] Another highly interesting case demonstrates this: the press reports the story of a confirmed atheist whose lectures used to keep the mullahs of the entire region in fear. Yet when he died the villagers buried him with the usual Moslem rites, and the selfsame mullahs whom he had reviled attended the funeral.[35]

The ideological conference at Dushanbe (see above) came to the conclusion that Islam is a menace because it fosters a sense of "national exclusiveness" among the population, and at a meeting of the Tadzhik Party Central Committee, First Secretary Rasulov stated that the Moslem clergy "play on national feelings and try to strike a blow at fraternal friendship among peoples."[36] At a similar conference in Makhachkala, the head of the Propaganda and Agitation Department of the Daghestan Oblast Party Committee stressed that "remnants of religious survivals are a hindrance to the cause of strengthening the friendship of the peoples."[37]

In answer to the question why Soviet Moslems still adhere to their religion one may point to deeply-ingrained custom and the powerful influence in Moslem society of the family as the conserver of tradition and the Islamic moral code. The young generation is still much more influenced by its parents than by the atheist attitude propagated by the state. A potent factor is also the will to resist attempts to break down Moslem national consciousness on the part of the authorities. Here Islam is felt by its adherents to be more than a religion. It is the essence of their entire national and cultural heritage.

---

[34] *Sovetskaya Kirghiziya*, January 9, 1966.
[35] *Ala-Too*, No. 7, 1965, p. 107.
[36] *Kommunist Tadzhikistana*, July 10, 1963.
[37] *Voprosy filosofii*, No. 5, 1961, p. 159.

Bibliography

Bennigsen, Alexander and Lemercie-Quelquejay, Chantal, *La presse et le mouvement national chez les musulmans de Russie avant 1920*, Mouton et Cie, Paris, 1964.

Hakimogly, A., "The Central Religious Administration of the Moslems in Russia and its Task," *Cultura Turcica*, Vol. I, No, 1, Ankara, 1964; "Forty Years of Anti-Religious Propaganda," *The East Turcic Review*, No. 4, Munich, 1960, pp. 67—69.

Hayit, Baymirza, *Turkestan im XX. Jahrhundert*, C. V. Leske Verlag, Darmstadt, 1956, "Islam im Russischen Imperium. Die Herausforderung des Islam," Musterschmidt-Verlag, Göttingen 1964, pp. 160—181; *Sowjetrussischer Kolonialismus und Imperialismus in Turkestan*, pp. 35—38, published by the Institut für Menschen- und Menschheitskunde, published in the Netherlands by P. H. Klop.

Institute Publications (1951—1962), published by the Institute for the Study of the USSR, Munich, 1963.

Karcha, Ramazan, "The Northern Caucasus," *Obyedinenny Kavkaz*, No. 1, Munich, 1964, p. 32; Nos. 2—3, pp. 45—47.

Kirimal, Edige, *Der nationale Kampf der Krimtürken*, Verlag Lechte, Emsdetten, Westfalen, 1952, pp. 19—25.

Pipes, Richard, "Muslims in the Soviet Union," *Islam and Communism*, New York, 1960, pp. 11—18.

Stackelberg, Georg von, "Current Soviet Policy Toward Islam," in *Religion in the USSR*, published by the Institute for the Study of the USSR, Munich, 1960; "Anti-Islamic Propaganda in the Soviet Union," *Bulletin*, No. 5, Munich, 1960, pp. 34—37;

Sultan, Garib, "Recent Developments in the Soviet Eastern Republics," *Islam and Communism, op. cit.*, pp. 19—25.

Jews and Judaism in the Soviet Union

Hans Lamm

It seems necessary to begin by clarifying the concept "Jews." Even in Western countries no universal agreement exists on the definition of the term,[1] yet in general Jews may be considered, and consider themselves, as a religious group that one can join and leave, like any of the Christian or other denominations. Some Jews have put more emphasis on a national concept of Judaism,[2] while others, not fully satisfied by either the religious or national definition, feel that something called a *Schicksalsgemeinschaft* (community with a common history) might be more appropriate.[3] While we need not enter into this discussion, we must still determine how the term "Jews" is applied in the Soviet Union.

In pre-Revolutionary days the Jews were discriminated against and their civil liberties were heavily curtailed by the Tsarist government. It is hard to determine whether this was done mainly on religious grounds or whether a part was played by the feeling that the Jews were a strange national minority.[4] In the Soviet Union today, Jews are required to declare themselves as being of Jewish nationality. In population surveys and statistics and when applying for identity cards, Jews have to put "Jewish" under the "Nationality" heading, whereas other citizens may write "Russian," "Ukrainian," "Armenian," "Georgian," or "German," etc. This is obligatory for all persons of Jewish descent, regardless of whether they belong to the Jewish religious community or not. Thus, Jews are compelled to declare as members of a Jewish nationality, whether they consider this appropriate or not. Question 5 in their identity card marks them as "Jews," something that will be disadvantageous to them in dealings with officials who have anti-Semitic leanings. It has recently been rumoured that the identification papers listing "nationality" are to be replaced by new ones without that column, but this has not happened yet.

No official Soviet figures on the number of Jews in the USSR have been released since the Census of 1959, when the figure given was 2,268,000. This has

---

[1] Cf. the book *Wer ist Jude?* by William S. Schlamm (Stuttgart, 1964), which, incidentally, has been rejected by most of its Jewish reviewers (e.g. N. P. Levinson and Hans Lamm in *Allgemeine Wochenzeitung der Juden in Deutschland*, Düsseldorf, October 16 and November 27, 1964).

[2] Cf. the famous sentence "Wir sind ein *Volk*, ein Volk" in Theodor Herzl's book *Der Judenstaat*, Vienna, 1896 (later editions in English and other languages have been published frequently since). Herzl's pamphlet has become the classic basis for the political movement of Zionism which aimed at and accomplished the creation of a Jewish national home in Palestine (Israel became a state, immediately recognized by the USA, the USSR and other powers, on May 15, 1948).

[3] Hans Lamm, "Von verschiedenen Arten der Gemeinschaft" in *Allgemeine Wochenzeitung der Juden in Deutschland*, March 18, 1960.

[4] See Prof. Salo W. Baron's work, *The Russian Jews*, New York, 1964. This is the most comprehensive study of the entire history of the Jews in Russia both before and after 1917. A further standard volume is Solomon M. Schwarz, *The Jews in the Soviet Union*, Syracuse, 1951. Quite recent is a book edited by Jacob Frumkin, Gregor Aronson and Alexis Goldenweiser, *Russian Jewry*, New York, 1966.

been the subject of much discussion, some assuming the number of Jews to be much higher, and others doubting that all who gave their nationality as "Jewish" really should be regarded as "Jews." At any rate, no other statistics are available, and the method used by the *American Jewish Year Book* to assume a rate of increase of the Soviet Jewish population identical with that of the Soviet population as a whole (thus reaching an estimate of 2,454,000 for 1963) is obviously problematic.

Soviet laws do not deal in any specific way with the Jews as a group or as individuals. Of course, Article 124 of the Constitution stipulates separation of church and state, as decreed by the Soviet government on January 23, 1918, and in Article 129 tribute is paid to the concept of national independence and self-determination. It has been shown in general that these principles are often mainly honoured in the breach,[5] and we shall have to ascertain how far this holds true with regard to the Jews.

This paper was completed after a stay in the USSR in April 1966, during which the cities of Kiev, Leningrad and Moscow were visited. In contacts with Jews and non-Jews an attempt was made to verify or correct the elaborate material, both academic and popular, available in large quantities in English-speaking countries.

The question as to whether the Jews as a group play a role in the spiritual life of the Soviet Union can only be answered in the negative. Individual Jews, probably more than might be assumed on the mere basis of numbers (the Jews constitute between 1 and 1.5 per cent of the Soviet population) make their contribution to the cultural and intellectual life of the country, but they do so as individuals and not as Jews.

In Tsarist Russia there were no openings in life for non-Christians, and hardly any even for non-Orthodox groups. This resulted from the semi-medieval nature of society, with its close interlinking of secular and clerical authorities. While in the relatively liberal and tolerant societies of Germany and other Central European and Western countries—including, of course, the United States of America— Jews as a religious or cultural entity could and did make their distinct contribution to the life of the larger community, nothing of that kind seems ever to have been possible in Russia. The emancipation granted to Jewry elsewhere in Europe in the 18th and 19th centuries did not occur until 1917, and after the Revolution they were to discover that their "liberation" was not only faulty but false.

The present situation of Jews in the USSR is examined below under several headings:

1. *Religious Activities :* As a religious group the Jews theoretically enjoy the same (limited) rights as other churches or sects. As has been noted, the Soviet Constitution does allow worship, but practically prohibits religious instruction,

---

[5] *Genocide in the USSR* (1958) and *Religion in the USSR* (1960), published by the Institute for the Study of the USSR, Munich. Both volumes contain largely identical papers on *The Jews* by Salomon Goldelman.

while anti-religious propaganda is encouraged. Therefore, believers are at a disadvantage *vis à vis* the atheists: the Soviet state, considering religion an undesirable and dangerous opiate, reluctantly tolerates worship by the faithful, whose number in the five decades of the regime's existence has diminished considerably and constantly.[6] Religious instruction to persons under 18 years of age may only be given in groups not exceeding three in number, thus banning all religious group instruction (which is traditional in European secular and in American parochial schools), yet permitting the training of some priests. All experts agree that (a) the Russian Orthodox Church does enjoy a privileged position for historical reasons as well as present-day politics, and that (b) the Jewish religious group is even less equipped with rights and opportunities to perform its traditional functions than other Christian sects or the Moslems. Soviet propaganda emphasizes that religious activities, in addition to the services in synagogues, have been permitted to an ever-increasing extent.[7] This claim is not completely borne out by the facts. True, the baking of *mazoth* (unleavened bread to be eaten during the eight days of Passover, the Jewish Easter) was permitted in 1965— after having been entirely prohibited in 1962—in large cities, e.g., those three which we visited, and in Odessa. But in some others it could not be performed since the local authorities have it in their power to grant—and therefore can withhold—such permits, and as no nation-wide policy nor authority seems to exist, no universal practice prevails either. This can be proven again with *Shehita*, the ritual slaughter of cattle to obtain the "kosher" meat which religious Jews consume. In Moscow such slaughter was taking place, but in another city that was mentioned to me, permission for a *Shohet* (the man trained to perform this ritual job) to move to that locality was refused, and thereby re-introduction of *Shehita* was frustrated. Also, the number of "operating" synagogues is steadily diminishing: the Chief Rabbi of Moscow, Yehuda Leib Lewin, mentioned in April 1965 that in addition to the fairly large synagogue on Archipova Street, two smaller ones were open to worshippers; another source stated that these two halls were too small to be really called synagogues. Be that as it may, the total number of worshippers accommodated in these three buildings must have been less than two thousand, a small fraction of the Moscow Jewish community.[8]

---

[6] The places of worship for Christians and Jews which we visited in the above-mentioned large cities during the Easter period 1966 were attended only by elderly people of about sixty years or over. Young people whom we observed crowding the Cathedral of Saint Vassily at Kiev around midnight on Saturday, April 9th, did so obviously out of curiosity or to annoy the minority of people present who desired to worship. Similar disturbances were reported from Moscow.

[7] See the booklet by Salomon Rabinovich, *Jews in the USSR*, published in Moscow in 1965.

[8] The Moscow Chief Rabbi, replying to my question, stated that it was "estimated" that 500,000 Jews were living in Moscow, but that he did not know whether this figure was correct or not. One could not help suspecting that he hesitated to commit himself one way or the other. What were the "right" answers to be given, or expected from him? Whom should he, as rabbi, consider "Jews"—those who were called Jews in their identity cards or those who believed in the God of their fathers and longed to pray to Him? This attitude of ignorance concerning basic facts of Jewish life could be found among Jews elsewhere, too. It seems justified to consider ᵗhis a symptom of frustration and possibly merely a vestige of Stalinist days, maybe more than that.

The question of Jewish prayer books (*Siddurim*) has for years been an issue in the discussions concerning Jewish religious life in the Soviet Union. In 1956 the late Rabbi Solomon Shlieffer announced that 3,000 copies of a prayer book had been printed for the first time in many decades. In the synagogues that we visited we could not discover a single copy, but only books dating from well before the Revolution. Some people claimed that those 3,000 copies had indeed been printed, but were shipped abroad to show how much the Soviet system had been liberalised. Even if this theory were disproved, could a token edition of 3,000 books be considered impressive or sufficient when Soviet statistics still speak of far more than 2,000,000 Jews? When we asked the present Chief Rabbi of Moscow about prayer books, he pointed to a pile lying at his side, replying: "With God's aid we are going to print; here you see the plates!" Press reports spoke of a projected 10,000 copies to be printed, but whether this is true and when it will be put into effect no one seemed to know. When we asked whether a *Yeshiva* (a school of higher Jewish learning where biblical and post-biblical literature and their commentaries are studied) was in existence in Moscow, we received an evasive answer. The usually well-informed *American Jewish Year Book* states in its volumes 59–66 that the *Yeshiva Kol Jacob* opened on January 6, 1957, and that it had thirty students the following year, sixteen in 1959, twenty in 1960, eleven in 1961, six in 1962, and five in 1963. The number of students in 1964 was not given. Others assured us later that this semi-academic centre had been closed. Yet, as is well known, hundreds of men are able to attend seminaries belonging to the Orthodox Church.

2. *Cultural Life :* Eastern European Jewry for many generations not only maintained its religious and charitable institutions, but likewise its own schools, periodicals, theatres, etc. All this belongs to the past. No permanent theatre performing in Yiddish (not to mention Hebrew) is to be found today anywhere in the Soviet Union, although occasional performances by small itinerant troups are permitted. We were privileged to see one by Anna Guzik and her colleagues in a medium-sized theatre hall (capacity probably slightly below 1,000) in Moscow. For one week they staged a dramatisation of stories by the well-known and highly popular author, Sholem Alehem (1859–1916). The audience, much larger than the groups of worshippers we had seen at the synagogues, was interspersed with some fairly young people of twenty-five or over who apparently understood enough Yiddish to be able to follow the play.[9] We were impressed by two small incidents during the performance: when the actor who played the part of Uriel D'Acosta (1590–1640) exclaimed with much pathos: "I wish to die as a Jew, as I lived like a Jew," an outburst of applause ensued, and after the play had ended (major parts of which were set in New York), the actors came in front of the curtain and sang the modern Israeli folk song "Habbana Gilah." Both events were, no doubt, meant as demonstrations of some kind of resistance, or at least of loyalty to the Jewish community, something which is frowned upon by the Soviet

---

[9] We were told that a reading from Sholem Alehem's works in Russian, which took place the same week, was not at all well attended. The poet's works are circulated in large editions (allegedly running into millions of copies) but not in the original Yiddish tongue, only in Russian translations!

rulers. Similar defiance has occurred elsewhere: we were told of Georgian Jews in or near Tiflis who refused to move when the authorities wished to close their synagogue, and who have succeeded in frustrating this hostile move for the time being.

The only two periodicals in Yiddish published in the Soviet Union are mentioned not so much to show that cultural life can flourish, but rather the opposite. In Moscow the *Sovetish Heymland* has been printed in an edition of 25,000 copies since July 1948. And still less significant is the small Yiddish newspaper in Birobidjan, only a few hundred copies of which appear.

3. *National Life :* In Soviet ideology two seemingly contradictory tendencies exist, dating from the early writings of Lenin and Stalin on the nationality question: to grant nations and national minorities independence and opportunities for national self-realization, and on the other hand to suppress national differences as outworn remnants of a bygone past and to submerge them in a unified communist society. In the case of Jews the latter tendency has for decades been predominant, less because the Jews wanted it so, but rather because the regime and its rulers demand the radical surrender of all group characteristics. Rabinovich expresses himself in favour of assimilation as the price of survival.[10] Whether he realizes it or not, this survival will be at best one of individuals born as Jews, not of Jews as a group. Thus, the Soviets fulfill with much more consistency than its French revolutionary author the demand: "To the Jews as individuals *all* rights— to the Jews as a group *none*." All the indications are that the Jews as a national group are given far less privileges than many much smaller nationalities. Nahum Goldmann pointed out in 1960 that 85 different books were published for 479,000 Maris, 97 titles for 369,000 Ostinims and 89 titles for 230,000 Yakuts.[11] In Germany, where only about one per cent of the number of Jews in the Soviet Union live, three Jewish weeklies and a number of irregular periodicals are published; and in the USA, where about twice as many Jews live as in the Soviet Union, the number of Jewish periodicals is now over 200.[12] Yet for the Jews of the Soviet Union, whose numbers undisputedly exceeded two million in 1958, not a single book was published in Hebrew or Yiddish.

While Jewish authors publish in Russian, books in Yiddish are printed very rarely: in 1959, 30,000 copies of selected works by Sholem Alehem were published in Yiddish on the occasion of the centenary of his birth in March 1959; A special 40 kopek stamp with his picture was issued by the postal authorities, without, however, the usual identifying inscription as to nationality and achievement. Statistics published in 1964 stated that between 1955 and 1961 only six books were published in Yiddish.[13] During this period, 187 books by Soviet Jewish authors were published; of the total of 11,931,630 copies, only 133,000 were

---

[10] Rabinovich, *op. cit.*, p. 40.

[11] Martin Buber & Nahum Goldmann, *Die Juden in der UdSSR*, Ner-Tamid-Verlag, Munich & Frankfurt, 1961. It is not know to this author whether Dr. Goldmann's observations, delivered in Paris, September 1960, have been printed in English too.

[12] *American Jewish Year Book* (hereafter *AJYB*), Vol. 66, New York, 1965, pp. 549—555.

[13] *Ibid.*, 1964, Vol. 64, p. 355.

issued in Yiddish (slightly over 3 per cent of the titles being published in Yiddish, and accounting for slightly over one per cent of the total copies published). *Sovetish Heymland* published in 1962 a list of 74 Yiddish writers active in the USSR, and in January 1962 the magazine sponsored a meeting of over 30 Yiddish authors. Meir Faerber, a writer living in Israel, reported recently that three books in the Yiddish language had been issued in the Soviet Union.[14] There was, however, no indication that they reached readers in Russia, and it may well be that they too, like many Soviet and East European postage stamps, were issued almost wholly for foreign consumption.

Up to 1948, Yiddish literature was printed and distributed widely in the Soviet Union; thereafter the publishing houses were closed, hundreds of authors imprisoned, and in 1952 many of them executed or exiled. Goldmann, like others, stressed that the Jewish group is not permitted a central organization such as most other religious groups (not only the Orthodox, but Moslems, Baptists and others also) possess. Even the few rabbis cannot meet any longer as a body to discuss problems and questions of common interest: their last joint conference took place in 1926. The Moscow Chief Rabbi has taken pains to emphasize that he is in charge only of the Jews in that one city. It is also swiftly becoming obvious that the synagogue buildings are not only of importance to those who desire to pray there. Since Jewish organizations other than the religious circles are not tolerated at all, we were frequently told: "If you want to meet Jews, you must go to the synagogue." To some extent they have taken over the function of club houses or community centres. Goldmann has referred to 60–70 synagogues available to Soviet Jews (of whom it was estimated that 1.5 million still had some religious interests), while Rabinovich maintains that the Soviet Union has 97 synagogues. Even if this figure could be proved correct, it would still be amazingly low.[15] What are three synagogues in Moscow compared with the 18 in Budapest or the 50 in Bucharest, a city which has nine Jewish schools, while none legally exists in the whole Soviet Union?

One can only speculate why even the few rights, liberties and opportunities granted to other national groups in the Soviet Union are not offered to the Jews, but there is no denying the facts. Russian Jews always had a stronger national consciousness than those in the West, who had to a high degree been assimilated by their non-Jewish neighbours following their emancipation late in the 18th, and early in the 19th century. Russian Jews therefore joined the Zionist national movement in large numbers and contributed heavily to its leadership.[16]

---

[14] *Münchener Jüdische Nachrichten*, Munich, May 13, 1966.

[15] In post-war Germany, with its mere 30,000 Jews, the number of functioning synagogues exceeds 50. In most communist countries the situation is much better than in the Soviet Union. Cf. Goldmann, *op. cit.*, pp. 35/36, and Hans Jörg Pommer, *Antisemitismus in der UdSSR und in den Satellitenstaaten*, Bern, 1963, Swiss Eastern Institute, Publication No. 15.

[16] The Russian Jewish physician Leon Pinsker (1821–1891) authored a Zionist "Self-Emancipation" programme (1882) long before Herzl even thought of Zionism. Other Russian Jews (Nahum Sokolow, Chaim Weizmann, David Ben Gurion) spent their early years in the Russian Empire, which they decided to leave.

It cannot be disputed that if the Jews are considered a national group, Zionism is a legitimate expression of their national aspirations. The Soviet regime has persecuted Zionism intensively for many years, and no Zionist groups have been permitted to be active on Soviet soil. The early waves of immigrants (*Aliyot*) to Palestine (then still a part of the Ottoman Empire) consisted largely of Russian Jews, but for decades emigration of Soviet Jews to Israel, or any other lands, has virtually stopped. While other countries in the Soviet orbit have allowed Jews to go to Israel in tens of thousands, no such development has been observed in the Soviet Union. A German journalist has given the following statistics on recent immigration to Israel by Jews from the Soviet Union:[17] 200 annually between 1960 and 1964, 800 in 1965 and 1,000 in the first three months of 1966. Even if correct, these statistics do not necessarily justify his conclusion that "there exist indications of a Soviet willingness to let those Jews go who desire to emigrate." We were told in Moscow that decisions to grant such permission are made at the local level and not, as one might assume, at the highest. It is futile to speculate how many Russian Jews would move to Israel or other countries if they had the opportunity, and it is hardly realistic to expect a marked relaxation of the emigration restrictions which have characterised the Soviet system for so long.

Zionism is described in Soviet propaganda as a reactionary and even imperialist bourgeois movement,[18] and the more the Soviet Union wishes to endear itself to the Arab states, which have declared their vehement hostility to Israel since her creation, the more it has joined in Arab attacks on Zionism and the young Jewish state created by Zionists. The importance attached by the Soviet leaders to cordial relations with the Arabs is demonstrated by Premier Kosygin's eight-day visit to Cairo during the first half of May, 1966. Whereas in 1948 the Soviets saw fit to support the United Nations plan to divide Palestine and thus to make possible the emergence of Israel, they have rather consistently shown hostility to Israel since then.[19]

4. *International Relations:* Experts agree that the Soviet leadership has for decades strongly supported Russian nationalism at the expense of an internationalist line. Distrust of international movements and tendencies has been a feature of the major phases in the regimes of both Stalin and his successors. Jews are rightly or wrongly considered "internationalists" and hence it was not only Nazis and Fascists who used to agitate against "international Jewry." The Jews of the United States, estimated to number five millions or more, are the largest

---

[17] Hans Ulrich Kempski, *Süddeutsche Zeitung*, Munich, May 14, 1966.

[18] Nahum Goldmann felt compelled in May 1966 to protest to Kosygin against anti-Israel statements made by the latter at the conclusion of his visit to Egypt.

[19] Speculations have often been voiced that the Soviets may relax their attitude toward Israel. A Jewish journalist, Gershon Swet, however, in the New York weekly *Aufbau*, June 10th, 1966, expressed his conviction that the visit by General de Gaulle to Moscow in June 1966 would not bring about a change of attitude towards Israel by the Soviet rulers. He even pointed out that the Soviets in their conflict with Red China—the only country that has recognized the rather spurious "Arab Army for the Liberation of Palestine" led by a certain Ahmed Shukairi—wish to out-do the Chinese in their pro-Arab and anti-Israel posture.

Jewish group in the entire world, and this fact helps to nurture Soviet hostility to the Jews, together with suspicion of any internationalism, as well as antagonism towards the "unreliable" Jews, who are considered "internationalist."

5. *Evidence of Anti-Semitism:* Do all these factors—negative attitudes toward Judaism as a religious, a national or an international phenomenon—amount to the conclusion that the Soviet system today is to be regarded as anti-Semitic? It is my conviction that this question cannot be clearly answered one way or the other. It should not be overlooked that a strong anti-Jewish tradition has existed in Russia and that it led to the terrible pogroms of the early 1880's and in 1903. The notorious remark by a Tsarist official in 1890 to the effect that the Jewish question could be solved only by letting one-third perish, baptising one-third and letting the remainder of the then five million Jews emigrate was not one man's private opinion but rather the expression of an attitude of large sections of the public and the Tsarist government.[20] There is no reason to assume that anti-Semitism in the USSR has vanished within the last half-century; indeed, there are many indications of its continued existence, although the official and proclaimed attitude is one of strong disapproval.[21] Many factors may lead to attitudes or actions which appear anti-Semitic, such as drives against profiteering, black marketing, or recalcitrant intellectuals, since in the public mind Jews are often identified with these phenomena of Soviet society. Yet it might be unjust to speak of anti-Semitism as if it were part of the Soviet system. There is no universal agreement on this question: a pamphlet published by the Socialist International[22] has claimed that anti-Semitism does exist, and has substantiated this claim by stating that Soviet citizens of Jewish birth are "not given the same freedom of religious worship and association as that which is accorded to citizens of other legally-recognised religions, not given the same opportunity as other nationalities to use the language of their preference in education and cultural life, not given protection like that accorded to other minority groups against manifestations of hostility and prejudice." It also denies that "citizens of Jewish origin enjoy equal opportunities with others for education and general prospects in society," and maintains that "Jews are being singled out in a special and prejudiced way which sets them apart from other nationalities."

If one reads the quotations from the book *Judaism without Embellishment*, published in Kiev in 1964, or looks at the cartoons reprinted in the pamphlet, partly anti-Jewish, partly anti-Israeli in character, and if one further keeps in mind that under a totalitarian system such as the Soviet, nothing can be published that contradicts officially-approved policy, one begins to doubt whether the Party and Government oppose anti-Semitism as strongly as they declare for foreign consumption from time to time.[23]

---

[20] Constantin Petrovich Pobedonostsev is reported to have voiced this view to Alexander O. Zederbaum (Cf. Baron, *op. cit.*, p. 59).

[21] See Pommer's book and others. (See Bibliographical Note.)

[22] Isi Leibler, *Soviet Jewry and Human Rights*, Melbourne, 1965.

[23] Cf. the oft-quoted Stalin interview of January, 1931.

6. *Suppression of Culture :* The term "genocide" has been used to describe Soviet policy towards the Jews, and it is true that at certain periods when disregard for human life was more prevalent in the Soviet Union than in recent years, Jews were killed by the thousands. Whether they met with their fate because they were Jews or because rhey were considered harmful for political, economic, ideological or cultural reasons, is a matter of conjecture. Today, this period belongs to the past. Lewis S. Feuer[24] has very aptly characterized the changed situation, and he comes to the conclusion that the Jewish people are allowed to exist, although their culture is being extirpated.[25] He speaks of "culturecide," not "genocide," and of "Jews on official sufferance" who are required to "suppress any Jewish identification," and concludes: "Jews in professional and intellectual life generally do well to avoid identifying themselves as Jews."[26] Feuer mentions that 500,000 Jews still speak Yiddish and that a systematic effort is being made to deprive them rapidly of this linguistic link which, in addition to the common faith, has bound them together effectively for centuries.[27] He further concludes that "assimilation"[28] is planned from above, directed from above, enforced through sanctions, and combined with refusal to make books and teachers available, which is in itself destructive of human freedom.[29]

One can hardly dispute that it belongs essentially to the cultural freedom of an ethnic minority not only to learn from its spiritual, intellectual and linguistic heritage, but also to communicate with members of the same minority in other places and countries. All this is being denied to the Jews in the Soviet Union. They lack an overall organization of any kind in their own state and know very

---

[24] Lewis S. Feuer, "From all Their Habitations" in *Judaism*, Vol. XIII, Winter 1964.

[25] If one examines the five definitions of "genocide" as given by Article II of the Convention on Genocide (approved unanimously by the United Nations General Assembly on December 9, 1948) and the broader ones given by the Soviet Union and quoted by Nikolai K. Deker in *Genocide in the USSR* (New York, 1958, pp. 1 and 2), one comes to the conclusion that both recent and present Soviet policy toward its Jewish minority cannot fairly be described as "genocide" any longer.

[26] Even in our comparatively short stay in the USSR, we had experiences with writers and interpreters who were Jews but who took pains not to reveal it. Our feeling was not so much that they were "ashamed" of their Jewish orgin, but rather eager to submerge in the great nation forming the USSR. They lack Jewish traditions and a sense of belonging to the Jewish group, such as the otherwise well-educated lady to whom we spoke and who professed complete ignorance when the "Book of Ruth" from the Bible was mentioned to her.

[27] Rabinovich (*op. cit.*) states, obviously with approval: "It is absolutely normal...that in the Soviet Union where the Jews enjoy full equality, both legally and factually, their natural assimilation should be a permanent process taking place most intensively. It is indicative that fewer and fewer Jews now speak Yiddish."

[28] Rabinovich replies to the question "Are Jews being assimilated in the USSR?" simply "Yes," and goes on to explain that the "striving to retain the specific features of Jewry" was the result of "the national oppression of the Jews" and of anti-Semitism, while assimilation was characteristic of "the most highly-developed countries of Europe."

[29] In a Moscow hotel and in a foreign literature bookshop, *Valley of Exile* by Ivan Olbracht (1882–1952), a Czech author, could be bought in English. The book contains three stories centering on orthodox Jews, their religious and social life. It seems unlikely that a Russian Jewish writer would be able to publish novels with similar subjects in the USSR in any language.

little even about Jews living in other regions or cities of the country;[30] they know even less about Jewry in other countries. There is practically no source available to them from which they can get information about their co-religionists or co-nationals, and news about the growth of the state of Israel is more than taboo. This tendency has lead to very strange results: in the synagogues which we visited, people were quite amazed that we could live unharmed in the Federal Republic of Germany (they had believed *Pravda* and *Izvestia* reports that the Nazis were still, or once again, in power there). The Rabbi of Moscow received Jewish periodicals from Poland and Rumania, but none from Israel, the United States or any other Western country. Still, he may have been slightly better informed than other Jews in the USSR about Jewish contemporary life: with pride he pointed to a pile of letters from abroad on his desk. For the hundreds of thousands of Soviet Jews, however, the reality is what Feuer quoted as the sadly-resigned words of an ordinary, anonymous Jewish man-in-the-street: "Isaiah wrote that a time would come when brothers and sisters would lose each other. This is the present—*Keine svyazi* (no connections)." There is no reason to assume that this situation is likely to be altered by the Soviets. While Moshe Rosen, the Chief Rabbi of Rumania,[31] was able to attend the most recent gathering of the Executive of the World Jewish Congress at Strasbourg (July, 1965), it is unlikely that his colleague in Moscow would ever be given such permission.

7. *Reactions to Soviet Policy toward Judaism and Jewish Life :* Jews and non-Jews in the Western world have for years voiced protests against the policy of suppression of Judaism as a religion, or of Jewish secular culture, and have directed appeals to the Soviets to grant the Jews at least the limited degree of liberty that other religious and national minorities in the Soviet Union enjoy. Naturally, such voices have been heard more frequently outside the Soviet Union than within its borders. Yet it should not be forgotten that in his famous poem *Babi Yar*, first published on September 19, 1961, as brave a man as the young Soviet poet Yevgeni Yevtushenko dared to challenge his fellow-citizens with regard to anti-Semitism as a living prejudice in contemporary Soviet society. While the poem, of course, is basically a protest against the incredible tortures inflicted by the Nazis on Jews (and also on Russians and Ukrainians) at Babi Yar, it is also a warning against the inhumanity of anti-Semitism wherever it raises its ugly head:

> Let the "Internationale" ring out,
> when the last anti-Semite on earth is buried.
> There is no Jewish blood in mine,

---

[30] When the Moscow rabbi, replying to my question on the fate of the Jews of Birobidjan, professed ignorance, he was probably not being quite frank. He did not consider it wise to admit the failure of this Soviet venture. The Jewish population still given in 1959 as 35,000, (*AJYB*, Vol. 61, p. 263) was quoted four years later as having dwindled to 14,269 (*AJYB*, Vol. 65, p. 268.)

[31] Rosen reported (*World Jewry*, Vol. VIII, No. 5, London, 1965) that the 100,000 or 120,000 Jews living in Rumania today "have 300 synagogues in which services are held morning and evening." He continued: "We publish a journal for religious Jews, now in its ninth year, in three languages—Hebrew, Yiddish and Rumanian—which is the only Hebrew publication in the whole of Eastern Europe." The contrast with the Soviet Union is only too obvious.

but I am hated by every anti-Semite as a Jew,
and for this reason
I am a true Russian.[32]

Statements on the problem by Jews and others residing in Western countries have been more explicit and comprehensive. The Executive Committee of the World Jewish Congress, meeting at Strasbourg in 1965, declared:

The Congress takes note of the growing concern among the Jews the world over and in the international community with the problems created for Soviet Jewry because it does not enjoy the religious and cultural rights and facilities essential for the maintenance and development of its distinctive Jewish group life, rights and facilities enjoyed by other religious and ethnic groups in the USSR.

The Executive Committee note with satisfaction that public expression has been given to this concern by liberal and progressive people and parties as well as long-time friends of the Soviet Union.

Their concern is manifestly motivated, like that of the World Jewish Congress, by the failure to recognise the inalienable right of the Jewish people in the Soviet Union to equality of status and treatment with other groups, be they ethnic or religious, territorially concentrated or dispersed. From this central failure flow all the disabilities to which Jewish life is subjected in its natural resistance to the forces making for involuntary assimilation.

We renew our earnest appeal to the Soviet Government to re-examine the situation of the Jewish minority in the Soviet Union with a view of making available to it the same facilities for self-expression and the exercise of the right of association as are applied to other minorities in the Soviet Union and to Jewish communities in other Communist countries.

Meeting the spiritual and cultural needs of Soviet Jewry would contribute to the solution of problems which have caused world-wide concern, and would strengthen the forces working for international understanding. We are reinforced in this view by the support given by Soviet spokesmen in the United Nations to the right of ethnic and religious groups to exercise the right of association on a local, regional and national basis, and to participate in international non-governmental organisations. [33]

This was essentially no more than a reiteration of the "Appeal of Conscience" which about 100 leading Americans had adopted on October 21, 1963, at the Carnegie International Center in New York:

Having heard careful and objective evidence about many aspects of the life of Jews in the Soviet Union, we are moved to express unanimously our grave concern and to make the following appeals:

---

[32] One need not assume that Yevtushenko has read Jean-Paul Sartre's *Portrait de L'Antisémite* (1945), and it is therefore worth noting how strikingly their conclusions are almost identical. Sartre ended his essays as follows: "No Frenchman will be free, as long as the Jews are not in full possession of their rights. No Frenchman will be secure, as long as one single Jew in France, *in the entire world*, must fear for his life."

[33] A more elaborate and specific resolution on Soviet Jewry was adopted by the Fifth Plenary Assembly of the World Jewish Congress at Bruxelles on August 9, 1966, "and the participants rose from their seats to observe one minute of silence in solidarity with Soviet Jewry."

We appeal to all those in the USSR who genuinely desire the eradication of the evils of Stalinism and who, with us, thirst for truth, justice and decency.

We appeal to the Soviet authorities to act in this matter on the basis of their own ideological, constitutional and legal commitments.

We fervently hope that the following specific steps may be taken:

1. Jewish education in all its forms should be permitted.

2. Jewish cultural institutions should be reopened and Jewish artistic life—literature, theatre, music, in Yiddish and Hebrew—should be allowed to develop fully.

3. Central institutions to serve the religious needs of Soviet Jewry should be installed, and obstacles to the performance of sacred rites should be removed.

4. Formal religious and cultural bonds with Jewish communities abroad should be allowed, official exchange visits permitted, and the right to make religious pilgrimages to the Holy Land granted.

5. Permission for Jews to leave the USSR so that they may be reunited with families in other lands from whom they have been separated, should be implemented.

6. The anti-Jewish character that so strongly colors the official campaign against economic crimes should be eliminated.

7. A vigorous educational campaign against anti-Semitism should be undertaken.

We issue this appeal in all solemnity as a matter of urgency and elementary decency. We cannot keep silent so long as justice is not done on this problem.[34]

Hardly a single non-Jew has expressed himself so consistently on this problem and appealed as often to the Soviets in this regard as has Bertrand Russell. He, more than others, could hope for an attentive audience, since he himself is not only a proclaimed atheist but an acknowledged friend of the Soviet Union. In 1963 he engaged in an oft-quoted exchange of letters with Khrushchev which, however, resulted in no change of views or attitudes on either side,[35] and on July 22, 1964, he wrote to the editor of *Sovetish Heymland*, concluding his appeal on behalf of the Jews "...they feel that they are denied the means of living a complete and satisfying life in the Soviet Union because they are denied the cultural facilities made available to all other national and minority groups..." Russell continued:

I write because I am concerned for justice and for the good name of the Soviet Union. Unless people who are concerned for both raise their voices, the cause of peaceful coexistence and the pursuit of peace and general understanding between peoples and nations will be harmed by silence.

It will be unfortunate for both the Soviet Union and the Jewish people if something is not quickly done to accord dignity and justice to Soviet Jewry.

---

[34] Sponsors of the Conference were the member of the U.S. Supreme Court, William O. Douglas, the Rev. Dr. Martin Luther King Jr., the late Senator Herbert H. Lehman, Episcopal Bishop James A., Pike, United Automobile Workers President Walter Reuther, the veteran writer Norman Thomas, and the author, Robert Penn Warren.

[35] Bertrand Russell wrote to Khrushchev on February 2, 1963, and the latter replied on February 21st, both letters being published in the Soviet press on February 28th, 1963. A further letter from Lord Russell in which he wrote: "I fervently hope that nothing will take place which obliges us to believe the Jews are receiving unjust treatment in contradiction of the law" (April 6, 1963) remained unanswered and unprinted.

Apparently Lord Russell does not feel that the Soviets have in any manner altered or modified their attitude since. This is evidenced by the following message, which he addressed early in 1966 to the World Union of Jewish Students:

The situation of Jews in the Soviet Union is one of those tragic anomalies that exercise the concern of those who are steadfastly opposed to the Cold War and seek greater understanding between the nations. The irony of this situation is that Soviet Jews, survivors of a people whose destruction was a priority of Nazi Germany's war aims, are still facing the problem of national survival.

In 1948 Stalin and his secret police executed the Jewish creative intelligentsia and totally destroyed Jewish institutions, publishing houses, schools, theatres and every vestige of national existence outside the synagogues. De-Stalinization has brought little improvement. Jews still have no schools, no national theatres and no secular communal institutions. Although restitution was frequently promised in 1956 and 1957, only token symbols of culture have been permitted—a handful of books in the Yiddish language published in small editions and exploited as reassuring propaganda abroad, one monthly Yiddish magazine, one or two amateur dramatic groups and a few touring Jewish singers. This represents the total cultural resources of three million people traditionally regarded as one of the most talented and creative Jewish communities in the world. A comparison with other Soviet nationalities exposes the basic injustice of their situation, for even the smallest national groups in the Soviet Union are given the opportunity to pursue a cultural, social and political life of their own denied to Soviet Jews.

Although the anti-religious campaign in the USSR is directed against all religions, it is prosecuted with exceptional severity against Judaism, and propaganda against the Jewish religion often assumes the character of racial anti-Semitism, as in the writings of Kichko, Mavatsky and Osepov. The closure of synagogues has been conducted ruthlessly. At the time of the October Revolution there were some 3,000 synagogues in the Soviet Union. By 1956, according to a Soviet report to the United Nations, only 450 remained. Since then a further 354 have been closed and many cities with large Jewish populations have no places of worship available at all. Religious life is additionally hindered by the denial to Judaism of essential facilities available to other recognized Soviet religions, to the extent that makes it impossible to practice Judaism with the freedom guaranteed by the Soviet Constitution.

It is particularly tragic that the Soviet authorities have still taken no steps to end the separation of members of Jewish families disunited in appalling circumstances during the Nazi war. As a result of repatriation agreements between the USSR and other Communist countries in Eastern Europe, most of these problems have been solved in regard to Poles, Rumanians and Germans who were allowed to resettle in their own countries, many Germans being permitted to join relatives in Western Germany. The one community which suffered most at the hands of the Nazis—the Jews—has many thousands of individuals in the USSR who have been waiting for more than twenty years to join their close relatives in Israel and other countries. Elsewhere in Eastern Europe Jews in similar positions have been allowed family reunifications. The Soviet Union, however, has granted exit permits only to a small number of mainly elderly persons. Soviet Jews have no opportunity to voice their feelings publicly and are dependent on the support of public opinion abroad. I am happy that students of British universities are engaged in this special effort to make the facts more widely known. Discrimination against Jews in the

USSR, like the persecution of dissident intellectuals, seriously impairs the development of the USSR as a true socialist society and hinders all who work for international co-existence.

In April 1964, twenty-four American Jewish organizations founded an assembly called The American Jewish Conference on Soviet Jewry, and in the autumn of 1965 they issued an *Interim Report,* entitled "Soviet Jewry Today" in which they pose the following questions:

> During the past year, a spate of events, large and small, has given rise to guarded hopes that the Soviet Union is changing its policy toward the Jews and that the situation of Soviet Jewry is undergoing fundamental improvement. Are these hopes grounded in fact? If so, to what extent and in what way? If not, what is the meaning of the events cited as concrete evidence of progress?

The Report comes to the conclusion:

> Moscow is vulnerable on this issue: it is susceptible to the pressure of world opinion. It does move in response to it. There is even some reason to suspect that there are elements in the Party and Government, and certainly in influential sectors of the intelligentsia, that are unhappy about Soviet policy toward the Jews and are prepared to re-evaluate it.

It is to be hoped that these twenty-four organizations expressing this guarded optimism had more and better sources of information available than the present writer, who fears that they may have fallen victim to wishful thinking or that they have adopted this attitude to encourage a change that has not yet taken place. In their demands for the future they are no less determined than other representatives of liberal thought and world opinion:

> All those elements will be expecting far more, however, than even a full-scale educational campaign against anti-Semitism, invaluable as that in itself would be. They will expect not token concessions or small shifts and vague promises, but a systematic reversal of the policy of forcible assimilation. They will expect the State-supported establishment, as is the case with all other such groups, of a network of communal institutions—schools, textbooks, rabbinical seminary, teachers institutes, centers of advanced learning, research institutes, courses and classes in Yiddish, Hebrew and Russian for the study of Jewish history, literature and values, a publishing house, a professional theatre, newspapers and journals, a nationwide religious center, social-cultural centers in all the urban areas of Jewish population (in the absence of a geographical-territorial-political base for the Soviet Jews).
>
> In short, civilized world opinion, and the best elements of the USSR, will expect of a Soviet society that is gradually evolving along more rational lines the eradication of the irrational factors that have hitherto determined policy toward the Jews, and the establishment of the communal institutions necessary to assure the continuity and secure the future of Soviet Jewry, so as to permit them self-realization as Jews, as citizens and as human beings.

8. *The Attitude of Soviet Jewry :* The most telling phenomenon in this complex situation is possibly the utter silence of Soviet Jewry. If one pursues the rich literature on the subject, one will hardly discover a voice that can be accepted as

the true and free expression of Jews in Russia today. Even if one does not take Rabinovich's pamphlet as a crude piece of political propaganda, one will note that it is the more telling when it keeps silent on certain points than when it speaks with elaborate eloquence. Nowhere does the author claim that Soviet Jews today can lead a free, unhampered religious or cultural life of their choosing, and it is this which is the major issue as far as outside critics are concerned.

No Soviet Jew with whom we talked or whose utterances we read (with the sole exception of the official functionary and government propagandist, Solomon Rabinovich) claimed that Soviet Jewry is actually leading the life it wants to lead. No Soviet Jew has expressed his approval or disapproval of the numerous and well-publicized appeals made on behalf of the group. One might assume that they agree with the protests, that they wish the same limited rights as other minorities, but that they do not dare to say so. One might also venture to think that they no longer care one way or the other. Feuer quotes one of his sources as saying: "A dog should not open his mouth." Is that possibly the general attitude of Soviet Jewry?

Professor Feuer, who seems to us a more realistic observer of the situation than many other Jewish authors, reached the conclusion that in ten or twenty years there will be no Jews left in the Soviet Union.[36] It is probable that he takes "a Jew" to mean not simply a person born of a Jewish mother or a person whose identity papers describe him as of "Jewish nationality," but some-one who considers certain Jewish traditions, religious, cultural or otherwise, as part of his set of values in life. How many of the two to three million Jews believed to be living in the Soviet Union today still retain a sense of such values and a feeling of belonging to the Jewish group? While there is no scientific evidence and no statistics to prove or to disprove any theory, it must be assumed that almost five decades of systematic de-Judaization carried on so consistently by the Soviet government have accomplished a great deal. We must expect that a large part of the young and middle-aged people of Jewish orgin do not feel "Jewish" any more and would not "return to the fold," even if they could do so without the slightest difficulty.[37] It may well be that the appeals and protests which the Soviet leadership has not been willing to heed or even to take note of would not bring about a major change in the attitude of Soviet Jewry, even if the Soviets were suddenly to radically change their attitude. Jewish and world public opinion has consistently acted as if a compact Soviet Jewry were in existence, filled with the ardent desire to be freed of its spiritual, civic and social chains. Hardly any evidence allows us to believe that such an assumption is realistic. There is much cause to

---

[36] In August 1966 the press reportet that 20 American rabbis who had toured Jewish congregations in the USSR for three weeks, had reached the conclusion: "Judaism in the Soviet Union is dying and there are no indications that it could be saved."

[37] The New York weekly *Aufbau* on June 3, 1966 reported that after two years of effort Mrs. Margot Klausner, an Israeli, could now enter the USSR "to produce a documentary film on the life of the Jews in the USSR." Her project was supported by the editor of the Yiddish paper *Sovetish Heymland*. No one can foretell whether the film will ever be completed and shown in Israel or any other Western country.

suspect that only a small remnant still cares for Jewish life and therefore hopes for "liberation" of this kind.

What of the future? Western observers, who consider freedom of conscience and of cultural and national activity as the prerequisite for a dignified and full life, will view the picture presented here as dismal and depressing, while Soviet ideologists, convinced that Jewish religion and Jewish culture in general hinder progress on the road to communism, do not share that standpoint at all. There are, or at least were some, however, who tend to take a view different from that of the overwhelming majority of organized Jewish opinion. For example, the German Jewish author Joseph Roth (1894–1939), admittedly an outsider in many respects, wrote in his book *Juden auf Wanderschaft* (Jews in Migration) in 1926:

> If the Jewish question is solved in Russia, it will be half solved in all countries. There are hardly any Jewish emigrants from Russia, but there exist Jewish immigrants into that country. The religious feelings of the masses are decreasing rapidly. The strong barriers of religion fall, while the weaker ones of nationalism can hardly replace them. If this evolution continues, the era of Zionism and that of anti-Semitism will be ended, and perhaps that of Judaism. Some will welcome such development, others will regret it, but everybody must view with respect the spectacle of one people freed from the shame of suffering and another released from that of maltreating, of the persecuted liberated from pain, and the persecutor from the curse which is worse than pain. This is the great achievement of the Russian Revolution.

Although neither sharing Roth's analysis of the situation nor his predictions, we have quoted him at length to demonstrate that from a Jewish point of view another position can be adopted, differing from the many others quoted above.[38]

In conclusion it is worth quoting in full a report that appeared in the *New York Herald Tribune* (Paris Edition) of June 16, 1966, because this dispatch shows which rumours concerning a change in the Soviet attitude towards Jewish culture, as expressed in Yiddish literature, are being currently tolerated or even initiated by the Soviet authorities. In reading and evaluating the report, the reader should keep in mind that, while censorship for foreign correspondents no longer exists, they know that they can be expelled for news stories cabled by them which are considered untruthful and/or harmful to the Soviet Government. It reads:

> A report published in London by the Soviet embassy that this country's Jewish population would be given sweeping new privileges has been officially disavowed as "premature."
>
> The report stirred the hopes of Westerners concerned about the treatment of Jews in the Soviet Union. It would have amounted to a dramatic reversal of the policy, in effect since 1948, of stifling Yiddish culture.
>
> There have been some breaks in that policy, such as the establishment of a Yiddish literary magazine several years ago and an increasing amount of itinerant Yiddish theater, but foreign groups argue that this is insufficient. The report that conditions for Jews would improve beyond these token gestures appeared in the London embassy English publication *Soviet Weekly* last week. It said:

---

[38] Pro-Soviet is also Lion Feuchtwanger's book, *Moskau 1937*, Amsterdam, 1937.

117

1. Jews in Moscow would be allowed an experimental Yiddish-language school, with the possibility that a network of such schools would be opened.

2. Yiddish-language writers in Kiev would be allowed to start a magazine.

3. A state Yiddish theater would be established in Moscow, and the amateur group in Vilnyus, capital of Lithuania, would be turned into a professional group with state backing.

4. A Russo-Yiddish dictionary would be published.

If true, the developments would have gone a long way toward ending complaints often voiced by Western groups, that Jews are officially discriminated against in this country.

The London embassy's report was contained in a dispatch by the *Novosti* press agency. *Novosti* operates as a kind of public relations arm of the Soviet government.

Yesterday the *Herald Tribune* asked *Novosti* for confirmation and amplification of the report, which was reprinted by the "Jewish Chronicle" in London.

Semyon E. Rabinowitz, *Novosti*'s editor in charge of Jewish and Israeli affairs, said he knew nothing about the reported decisions to establish a Yiddish-language school or publish a dictionary. He said the reports on the other two decisions— regarding theaters and the magazine—were premature. He indicated, however, that something was in the offing on these points.

It is not unusual for Soviet officials to make statements to foreigners about new privileges for Soviet Jews and then find that the privileges are long in coming or never come at all.

Bibliographical Note

The B'nai B'rith International Council, 1003 K Street, N.W., Washington, D.C. published in August 1964 a survey entitled "The Status of Jews in the Soviet Union," and later an undated comprehensive study, "The Legal Position of the Jewish Community of the Soviet Union."

The American Jewish Committee, 165 East 56th St., New York 10028, N.Y. has mimeographed a "Selected Bibliography on Soviet Jewry."

The American Jewish Conference on Soviet Jewry, 55 West 42nd Street, New York 10036, N.Y., has published "Soviet Jewry Today" (An Interim Report).

Jews in Eastern Europe is a valuable periodical published quarterly by European Jewish Publications, Ltd., 83 Charlotte Street, London W. 1, England. *Focus on Soviet Jewry* is a newsletter issued at 145, Gray's Inn Road, London W. C. 1.

Congress Bi-Weekly the Journal of the American Jewish Congress, 15 East 84th Street, New York 10028, N.Y., frequently contains articles on Soviet Jewry and its problems, e.g., the issues for September 24, 1962; October 21, 1963; October 12, 1964; November 15 and 29, 1965, December 13, 1965; January 24 and April 4, 1966 (the latter five have particularly well-informed reports by S. L. Shneiderman) of May 9 and June 20, 1966.

It is noteworthy that many books on Russia that in no way concentrate on the Jews stress their unhappy fate, e.g. Henry Kolarz, *Verwandte in Moskau*, Düsseldorf, 1963, contains a chapter entitled "It is not easy to be a Jew in Russia" (pp. 243–256). Among other things, the author emphasizes the apprehensive attitude of Jews who do not dare to give their names. Cf. the book by Eric A. Peschler, *Privat in Moskau* (1966) also published by the Econ-Verlag.

Students particularly interested in the post-war period will benefit from consulting the following publication, which contains 845 items: *Jews in the Communist World. A Bibliography, 1945–1962* by Randolph L. Braham and Mordecai N. Hauer, Pro Arte Publishers, New York, 1963.

The Significance of Religious Themes in Soviet Literature

Zinaida Shakhovskaya

Simone de Beauvoir once asked the Soviet poet Andrei Voznesensky how he explained the lively interest in poetry displayed by the Soviet public. He answered: "Those who do not understand that the religious feelings of the Russian people are oriented towards poetry understand neither Russia nor Soviet poetry."

These words bring to mind another very different Soviet writer—Aleksandr Tvardovsky—who, when defending Yevtushenko and young writers in general, made the remark: "They are suffering from their youth, there is still something childish in them. They lack culture. And besides, you know, the icon has been removed from its place in the corner of the room and now that corner is bare."[1]

It is no easy task to discuss the religious questing in Soviet literature, since the whole approach is veiled: writers express themselves with considerable caution and have to some extent to practice self-censorship. It is up to the reader to read between the lines, and of course the Soviet reader is quite adept at this. One may safely say that not many people in the Soviet Union are completely indifferent to the issue of religion. Did not Aleksandr Blok write in his *Confessions of a Pagan* : "But I am a Russian, and Russians have always thought about the Church. Very few are completely indifferent to it. Some hate it very much, while others love it. Both sides with passion."[2] This is why there are fewer neutral, dispassionate books on the subject than in the West, where people are generally indifferent toward metaphysics. The Russians are not rationalists by nature, and that empty space in the corner of the room has to be filled. It is plain that the Lenin Corner[3] has not done so. It is a wonder that the words "God," "soul," and "immortality," for which there has been no place in the official Soviet ideology for decades, should still survive, when children are not allowed to receive a religious education. Yet books with such titles as *Not by Bread Alone* or *The Redemption* are published in the Soviet Union; a young poet has written a poem called "Isaac and Abraham," a Soviet general crosses himself before meals, a civil servant says, "Man proposes, God disposes," and the former Soviet Premier, Bulganin, comments when offering some caviar to a foreign diplomat that it is the best food ever created by God for man.

The Party authorities still do their best to root out the "religious survivals," as they call them, and the press returns again and again to the "accursed problem" of how to make Soviet man a thorough-going atheist.

---

[1] Jean Blot, "Entretiens avec Tvardovski," *Preuves*, Paris, February 1966.

[2] A. Blok, *Sochineniya* (Works), Vol. VI, Moscow-Leningrad, 1962, p. 39.

[3] *Leninsky ugolok*, a room in a club, school, factory, or office for studying the life and works of V. I. Lenin.

In 1964 and 1965 the journal *Science and Religion* repeatedly sought an answer to the question of how to expunge spiritual searchings from man in general, and from Russians in particular. It admits that this aspect of man's nature is something with which the ideologists must come to grips: "It is impossible to ponder on the meaning of man's life while avoiding its philosophical problems. They are justly called eternal."[4] What Soviet anti-religious literature sets out to do is to create a system of ethics without metaphysics, that is, to deny God but to avert a state of nihilism, which would certainly not suit the regime.

The interest of many Soviet writers in spiritual questions is indisputable. One of Pasternak's favourite books was *O lyubvi k Bogu i Cheloveku* (On Love for God and Man) by Archbishop Ioann San-Francisco, and now this book is in the hands of one close to the poet. While on a visit to the West, a Soviet poet gave a recital by heart of some of the verse in this book, commenting, "I often read it; it's good." Kirill Dmitri Pomerantsev has given me permission to quote from letters he has received from Soviet correspondents. One letter reads: "All genuine art is always religious. Rublev, Dostoevsky and Tolstoy are the trinity in our national art. The world finds them interesting only because they tried to solve the religious problem in the Russian way." Another reads: "Send me Berdyayev. Although his religious mysticism is foreign to me, there is much of interest in him. He illuminates Christianity from a viewpoint entirely unknown to us here."

Most of the letters I receive from Soviet listeners are in response to my broadcasts about Blaise Pascal and Georges Bernanos.[5] One listener wrote: "Don't tell us about Triolet and Aragon; we know them without your help, but without you we would not have known of Bernanos." The letters from a listener with a university education serve to illustrate how Soviet citizens use Aesopian language to get past the censor. He was grieving over the loss of his mother, whose name was Vera (Faith). In his first letter he wrote: "She bore her name with courage," then five months later he wrote: "My mother has left me to live with her 'credo,' which she wanted me to have and had silently bequeathed to me... I must grasp the source of her spiritual wealth; perhaps even a lifetime is insufficient for this. Today is Sunday, the day of rest. I am listening to a record of Bach's Agnus Dei..." This is how Soviet people write. And this is how Soviet authors write for their readers.

The Soviet authorities would like to place a new kind of barrier in the path of this growing spiritual movement in order to thwart the interest shown in religious matters by many, mainly writers, who are not well versed in theology. For this reason censors are allowing the works of such modern Western metaphysical humanists as Sartre and Teilhard de Chardin to enter the country. There is now even a Soviet specialist on de Chardin who writes in philosophical journals. De Chardin himself once said: "I am neither a philosopher nor a theologian, I only study 'phenomena.' I am a physicist in the old, Greek sense of the word." And after his death we witness a strange phenomenon: the French communist,

---

[4] *Nauka i religiya*, No. 7, 1965, p. 7.

[5] The author works for the French National Broadcasting System.

Garodi, asserts that Father de Chardin's ideas corroborate Marxism, freemasons claim that his ideas proclaim the autonomy of science, and even the Gaullist press sees him as its ideologist. The Vatican, however, is far from conferring its blessing on all of de Chardin's ideas. This gives a clue to the reason why some of these ideas are acceptable to Soviet anti-religious propagandists. Taking the lesser of two evils, they prefer Chardin to more orthodox Christian thinkers, after, of course, refashioning his ideas to meet their own needs. In their Marxist version, de Chardin's Christian cosmogony becomes a cosmogony without Christ, and his "world energy" loses its divine origins and divine sense of completion.

The Soviet reading public is keen to get hold of Berdyaev, Rozanov and Solovev, writers whom the state views with disfavour, and the young have recently begun to regard Dostoevsky as a mentor. Ilya Glazunov, a young and outstanding artist, writes:

> It appears to me that the brothers Karamazov are the personification of the ideas which fashioned the spiritual life of Russia . . . The problem posed by Dostoevsky is difficult, complex and tormenting, like tortuous gropings for the meaning of life, understanding of good and evil, the secrets of the human soul and universal brotherhood . . . Dostoevsky's main idea is the secret of man's being, which tormented the great writer all his life . . . Dostoevsky teaches us to be realists in the highest sense of the word, that is, "to look for man in man," in everyday life, to feel the mighty march of time with its eternal and fierce fight with good and evil, where the field of battle is the human heart.[6]

In the Soviet Union a book only appears in a large edition if it enjoys the approval of the authorities. Anti-religious novels such as *Teni ischezayut v polden* (The Shadows Disappear at Noon) by Anatoli Ivanov, and *Bog, Mister Glen* (God, Mister Glen) by Yuri Korobkov, appeared in editions of 200,000 and 100,000 copies respectively, whereas a "doubtful" novel only appears in 5 or 10,000 copies. Also, most of the officially-sponsored books of this propaganda type are crude in plot and style. To illustrate: *Bogi skhodyat na zemlyu* (The Gods Descend to Earth) by Vladimir Rozanov, published in 1966, describes "the putrid world of the followers of a cult which stretches out its mesh of lies and feigned compassion." It has all the typical ingredients: the beautiful daughter of a Party member is caught in the web of the Seventh Day Adventists. The pastor had sided with the Fascists—he is a confidence man, hypocrite and swindler. The pastor's son decides to join the Orthodox Church, since it is more profitable. His father shares his sentiments. The general impression given by the author is that the Adventists have been invented by the American bourgeoisie in order to poison the rank and file workers of the United States with religion. These hack works are just a part of the anti-religious campaign, a description of which is to be found in a pamphlet entitled *Situation Religieuse en URRS*, published in Brussels in 1965 by the Foyer Chrétien Oriental. The reason for this revived assault is given in the Soviet press: "The Church is advancing, the Church is reviving."[7]

---

[6] *Molodaya gvardiya*, No. 10, 1965, pp. 130, 132.
[7] *Komsomolskaya pravda*, February 6, 1965.

Hence the new spate of propaganda, such as the pamphlets "Without God the Road is Broader," "I Believe Because it is Absurd," and "Easter"; atheistic films with the titles, "Black Procession," Midnight Mass," and "Lo! Miracles!" The theatre is being enlisted too: in Odessa the "Atheist" theatrical group put on plays called "Light Conquers the Darkness" and "Without a Cross," and there are even anti-religious ballets and "popular, atheist concerts," 15,000 of which have already been held. If it is necessary to wheel such heavy artillery into battle and train it on religious targets, the victim must be quite lively and troublesome.

Anti-religious literature does not always achieve its aim: for instance, V. Tendryakov's atheist stories, "The Miracle-Worker" and "Something Extraordinary," are double-edged weapons. In the former the reader's sympathies could easily not be on the side of the rural school-teacher who draws a girl away from her faith. And in "Something Extraordinary" the reader's interest may centre on Aunt Sima and her spiritual gentleness, or on the personality of the mathematics teacher who came out in favour of the "lyricists," governed more by emotions than reason. It is no accident that *Nauka i religiya* suspended publication of Tendryakov's work, and rumour has it that his latest story, submitted to *Novy mir*, still has not been approved.

G. Kelt, a West Ukrainian atheist, has written an interesting criticism of the Soviet "Association of Militant Atheists" and its affiliate, the "Society for the Dissemination of Political and Scientific Knowledge." Commenting on the utter failure of atheist propaganda in the Soviet Union, she writes:

> Today we are again lulling ourselves to sleep: "many believers in our country have abandoned the Church and religion," we say. This is self-deception. One thing is true: in most parts of the Soviet Union there are neither churches nor cult members, but there are believers. If not Orthodox, then followers of the most diverse sects ... Closed parishes do not change believers into atheists. On the contrary, it heightens their inclination for religion and embitters them.[8]

Kelt also reminded her readers that even the most adamant atheists returned to the Church as soon as places of worship were opened during the last war. Moreover, she insists, "religion is no hollow fantasy of the mind. It has been created and nurtured through the course of centuries." In Shuya, which in terms of anti-religious education may be called a "model town," of 30,000 persons interviewed (eighty per cent of the population), ten per cent admitted that they were believers.[9] If this is representative of the USSR as a whole then there should be nearly 23,000,000 persons in the Soviet Union who openly profess religious beliefs. The Soviet press itself states that the percentage of believers is larger in the rural areas, and other Soviet sources indicate that believers of all persuasions number more than 100,000,000 persons.[10] To the extent permitted by the conditions under which writers in the Soviet Union labour, an attempt is made to give expression to these religious feelings. This is mainly done by means of refe-

---

[8] *Ibid.*, August 15, 1965.

[9] *Kommunist*, No. 15, 1965, pp. 59—60.

[10] *Nauka i religiya*, No. 10, 1965, p. 11.

rences to Russia's past and the spiritual values that informed it. The artist Glazunov, whom we have quoted above, recalls Pushkin's words: "Only savages
devour their own forebears."[11] And in an article in the press it is written: "A man
who has lost his memory is seriously ill and maybe incurable. The same applies to
a nation."[12] The Party authorities recognise that the interest in religion is closely
bound up with revival of interest in the past and in traditions. This urge on the
part of the young to revive time–hallowed traditions is reflected in the underground literary organization called SMOG, from the initial letters of the Russian
words *smelost, mysl, obraz, glubina,* meaning Daring, Thought, Image and Depth.
Its aim appears to be reconciliation of existentialism with the traditions of old
Russia.

In 1965 the Komsomol press organ *Molodaya gvardiya* launched a campaign to
preserve old historic buildings which quickly received the support of writers,
architects and historians, all anxious to see the cultural heritage saved from obli-
teration. Forced to take heed of this demand, but fearing that revival of interest in
the past for the first time in fifty years may cause the people to question official ideological values still more, the authorities are doing their best to emasculate the
culture of a by-gone age. Their spokesmen have zealously begun to "shape" the
culture of pre–Revolutionary Russia in the required mold. These efforts have
aroused anger, and one writer, Lev Lyubimov, has protested against the attempt,
for instance, to turn the famous 14th century Russian icon-painter, Andrei Rublev,
into an agnostic. "It must be conceded openly," he writes, "that the faith of
these simple men was genuine. Their faith, their craving, was strong and ardent,
so their works are truthful...and have the power to move the most confirmed
atheist."[13]

An even heavier rebuff came in a poem by Boris Slutsky:

> No, you can't thrust everything into a single mold.
> And however much you try,
> Rublev, who donned the habit of an ascetic monk,
> was hardly an atheist.
> And he was saved not by
> a herdsman of oxen,
> the symbol of labour,
> but by the Redeemer, the Redeemer,
> the Redeemer.[14]

The role played by the Church in Russia's history is treated quite unabashedly
in some Soviet historical novels. For instance, although in his novel "Ivan The
Third," Yazvitsky attributes some degree of free-thinking to the Prince of Mus-
covy, he speaks with surprising reverence about the role of the Church and depicts the old Orthodox way of life. And in 1962 a book on the first Russian printer,

---

[11] *Molodaya gvardiya,* No. 10, 1965, p. 93.

[12] *Literaturnaya gazeta,* June 24, 1965.

[13] *Novy mir,* No. 9, 1965, p. 205.

[14] *Yunost,* No. 2, 1962, p. 41.

Ivan Fedorov, appeared in which the latter's joy is described as he sees the Metropolitan Makari place the cap of Vladimir Monomakh upon the head of Prince Ivan. After such passages a young reader might want to go to church just to see what goes on there. Another character in the novel says to Fedorov that perhaps life is easier for a man if he is illiterate, to which Fedorov replies that it is always easier to live without thinking: "If you don't know of the behests in the New Testament, naturally there can be no sorrow that no one observes them."

In his book *Russkoye narodnoye tvorchestvo* (The Creativity of the Russian People) written in 1959, Chichegov includes "the Christian legends" in Russian folk-lore, because in his view the people did not adopt the saints in an abstract way, but wove their conception of them into everyday life and work.

An interest in religion may also be awakened by books on art which, although making the obligatory disparaging references to the "uneducated" artists of old Russia, nevertheless, when discussing a famous picture by Rublev inspired by a religious theme, refer to "angels with golden hair from the silent cell of the painter monk which are the image of humanity and imperishable, ageless beauty, purity and youth. And maybe someone reading about Rublev and the churches in Novgorod might reflect on why it is that these "uncultured" believers of the past were so far in advance of cultured Soviet contemporaries who created the Palace of Soviets and portraits of Stalin.

In Soviet fiction one may see how the living word and secret emotion break through all restrictions. More and more inspiration is being drawn from the past, which still lives in the Russian landscape with its age-old features—the little church and the belfry. In his book *Liricheskiye povesti* (Lyrical Tales), the noted writer, Vladimir Soloukhin, quotes another famous author, Efim Dorosh, who once said: "The Russian landscape—its plains scattered with hillocks, gullies and woods, will be poorer for the disappearance of the wooden churches that fit so astonishingly well into nature."[15] In his stories Soloukhin shows us in passing how the way of life of the peasantry is still influenced by Christian traditions: a young woman is hurrying to grind white flour for Whitsun; a passer-by, noticing that the director of a state farm was hiring youngsters to hurl nests containing fledgelings to the ground, angrily inquires: "What sort of a man is he? Has he never been baptized." And an equally well-known author, Solzhenitsyn, writes:

> When travelling the country by-roads of Central Russia you begin to understand what lies at the heart of the peaceful Russian landscape. It is the churches. Running up the knolls, ascending the hills, princesses in red and white, coming out to the wide rivers, with well-proportioned bell towers, tapered and carved, rising above the commonplace thatch and plank buildings, they reach upward to the heavens . . . And you are never alone: you approach a village and discover that the dead, the slain greet you from afar. The evening chimes rang out and floated over the village, over the fields, over the forest . . . It was a reminder to him that one must abandon petty earthly affairs and devote an hour and one's thoughts to eternity . . .[16]

---

[15] Vladimir Soloukhin, *Liricheskiye povesti* (Lyrical Tales), Moscow, 1961, p. 492.
[16] *Grani*, No. 56, 1964, p. 10.

Nature itself in Central Russia, its melancholy and monotony, induces a kind of serenity in man, and the townspeople, from time immemorial linked with the land, find solace from the soullessness of the cities during their vacations in the open spaces of the countryside. And there, having escaped the dull existence of Soviet everyday life, they sense the age-old soul of Russia, and suddenly a call from their ancestors wells up in their hearts, causing them to yearn for something not of this world.

I shall not here discuss the similar tendencies to be found in the literature of the non-Russian Christian peoples of the Soviet Union. A good outline is given by R. Modesto in an article that appeared in the January 1964 issue of *Russia Christiana*. It would appear that in both Georgian and Armenian literature, which is less heavily controlled by the central censorship authorities, there is more opportunity to write about God and things spiritual. Iraklii Abashidze has called one of his poems "The Garden of Gethsemane," and another bears the title "A Voice from the Church Porch." In the Ukraine, too, the poet Leonid Pervomaisky is one of those who write verse in which he uses symbolism to express his belief in God, and the works of the Belorussian writer, V. Korotkevich, contain elements of mysticism.[17]

Islam is an integral part of the culture and traditions of the Moslem peoples of the Soviet Union, and this ancient heritage still colours the outlook of many contemporary writers. The Kazakh poet, Oldzhas Suleymenov, who may in some ways be compared with Yevtushenko, entitled a poem "Prayer to Allah," and the Tatar author, Kuzmin, affectionately describes how the Moslem holiday of *Namaz* is celebrated in his native republic.[18] There are many other similar examples.

Among the Russian Jewish poets whose work contains particularly strong religious elements, the names Boris Slutsky and Iosif Brodsky spring to mind. And Nikolai Zabolotsky wrote the following in the 1950's:

> In the enchantment of a Russian landscape
> there is a genuine happiness, but it
> is not revealed to everyone, and is not even
> visible to every artist.
> . . . .
> The whole world is afire, translucent and spiritual.
> It is now that it is truly good.[19]

Zabolotsky writes of how he suddenly sees the image of Skovoroda in motionless stone, and feels that this philosopher of humanity's freedom and God's truth is near to him. In his collected verse we come across a poem entitled "Flight into Egypt," part of which runs:

---

[17] *Polymya*, No. 5, 1962, pp. 15–90; No. 6, 1962, pp. 45–96.

[18] *Prostor*, No. 6, 1963.

[19] N. Zabolotsky, *Stikhotvoreniya* (Poems), Washington-New York, 1965, p. 190.

125

> An angel is the guardian of my days...
> And in this unclear world,
> in this iridescent flame
> souls, angels, and children
> played to me on pipes.[20]

And in his "Conversation About the Soul" Zabolotsky writes:

> The peasants, breathing valour,
> gather in a group,
> and discuss where the soul is.[21]

Soloukhin has written a story called "Varvara Ivanovna," in which the main character is an old peasant woman, the mother of the brigade leader on a collective farm. The author describes the scene when she lies dying: "The room is tidy, there are flowers in pots, and the icons are draped with embroidered cloths and have small red lamps in front of them. The son is rebuked for allowing icons in his house, especially as he is a Party member and on the kolkhoz administration. "You ought to be ashamed!" they say. But the son retorts calmly: "Mama is dying," and adds defiantly: "Yesterday she received the last rites of the church."

A respect for the heritage of the past and a new-found sense of history are the unexpected themes that have been cropping up recently on the pages of the press. Such patriotic passages as the following occur:

> Our homeland resembles a huge tree... but all trees have roots. Roots are what we lived on yesterday... They are our grandparents and forefathers. They are their work, silently living side by side with us, in the stone images of the steppes, in wood carvings, wondrous churches, and splendid songs and fairy tales.[22]

The old and time-hallowed is contrasted with modernity in an article written by Lazar Karelin about a church that has been turned into a club:

> However many signs there may be of the new life, this church-club with its crossless cupola, the hoarding by the entrance, and these former cells fitted with new doors and window-frames, and the power transformer erected quite recently— despite all this, something venerable, calm, enigmatic and monastic still lingers here, reigning over everything, even, so it seems, in the air.[23]

In a prose work, Olga Berggolts lovingly describes the white cathedral at Uglich in the days of her childhood. Its image fills her heart with a premonition of happiness and joy; words that she frequently uses are "uplift in prayer," "ecstasy" and "contemplation." She also describes the death of her grandmother with emotion because the latter is fearless in the face of death, and this causes her to ponder that death does not really exist and can cause no terror.

Religious sentiments, metaphors and figures of speech may be found here and there in the works of many young and middle—aged poets who grew up under

---

[20] *Ibid.*, pp. 161—162.
[21] *Ibid.*, pp. 207—208.
[22] *Komsomolskaya pravda*, June 4, 1965.
[23] *Nash sovremennik*, No. 10, 1965, p. 18.

the Soviet regime. In his poem about Suzdal, Andrei Voznesensky links the image of this ancient Russian town with the Easter holiday. He speaks of honeycombs that gleam like icons, and of how in Suzdal the poet lives in Russia among the snows and the saints. In another poem on unrequited love, he implores the Madonna of Vladimir to mediate between him and his beloved, stressing that he is beseeching out of despair and not blasphemy. In Yevtushenko's poetry, too, there is religious imagery; he tells of his spiritual torments in which he finds weakness, holiness and sweetness, and appeals directly to God. In another poem he says that God cries out in him from the depths of his soul and that perhaps without this miracle life would be calmer and easier to live. Then he writes about tiring days when all kinds of people come to see him but never those for whom his heart yearns. He wants to speak to "somebody" who is capable of removing this estrangement of hearts which so troubles him. To judge by the context and metre of the poem, the Russian word for "Lord" would fit better than "somebody," and it is possible that this is what Yevtushenko wrote in his original version.

One of the most recent examples of this type of verse, once again with a symbolic church as the leitmotif, is contained in Soloukhin's now well-known poem "A Fairy Tale," in an anthology of his work called "To Live on Earth":

> Crunchingly the columns collapsed,
> and all the flanges fell asunder like ears of grain,
> the bricks crumbled into dust,
> the stones were turned into sand,
> the rains washed the gilt away.
> The icons were carted away to the school for firewood.

But before the demolition:

> In that temple, behind the heavy icon frame,
> behind the little ruby eye of the lamp,
> the Mother of God has been grieving for five centuries.

This icon was saved from destruction by an old woman who hid it in her hut. Many people tried to persuade her to hand over the icon to a museum:

> I told them: "Cut me up into little pieces,
> put out my eyes with red-hot iron.
> Mother of God, Holy Mary,
> I will not surrender her to the demons for desecration.[24]

The above are just a few instances of the writing in this vein that may be discovered in contemporary Soviet poetry and prose. One could also mention Yuri Stefanov, who mourns over his native soil:

> Oh, Lord God,
> hear my prayer.
> I know that Thou too
> art grieving with me.....

---

[24] V. Soloukhin, *Zhit na zemle*, Moscow, 1965, pp. 49—54.

And he casts himself in the role of a cleansing victim:

> The slippery steps
> I silently descend
> to Russia in Gehenna,
> to Russia in hell.
> ....
> And the tears and rottenness
> you can wash off, Russia,
> with my blood.....
> ....
> Ascend to the stars
> in glory and in vigour.
> I shall remain in hell
> instead of Russia.[25]

It would be difficult to find such an abundance of religious allusions in contemporary French literature, or in any other Western European writers. This applies equally to works published legally in the Soviet Union and to those which because of their excessively daring nature form part of the "underground" literature that occasionally finds its way abroad. Plentiful religious overtones may, for example, be found in an anthology of these "underground" poets published in the West. One poem reads:

> God will help me seek out the Motherland
> that I have lost.
> She is neither of the peasant nor of the
> sovereign lord —
> For me from times immemorial
> all Russia is the glow of God,
> a golden, schismatic blaze![26]

And another poet calls on:

> My holy and dishonourable people:
> pray and set off on your last campaign
> out of wrecked and ruined Russia.[27]

Yesenin Volpin writes:

> Icon lamps glimmered in the silence.
> A girl lay amidst flowers
> in the centre of the lofty church.

And as an antithesis to this serene Christian death:

> In the stagnant water there lies
> like a pole
> the shoeless corpse of a soldier...[28]

---

[25] *Grani*, No. 59, 1965, pp. 58–59.
[26] *Sovetskaya potayennaya muza* (The Secret Soviet Muse), Munich, 1961, p. 27.
[27] *Ibid.*, p. 89.
[28] *Ibid.*, p. 113.

The poem "Unfinished Song," by M. A. Narits-Narymov echoes the words in the Holy Scriptures, "blessed are the meek," and the Christian belief that evil is not eternal.[29]

I have deliberately left till the very end three outstanding Soviet writers, Boris Pasternak, Iosif Brodsky and Anna Akhmatova, who have served as an inspiration to so many of the new literary generation by the humanity and depth of feeling in their verse. Pasternak's poems "On Holy Thursday," "The Christmas Star" and "The Miracle" have left an abiding impression on all who have read them, and in Moscow in 1956 they were passed reverently from hand to hand. Brodsky was a close friend of Akhmatova, and when one reads his poetry one understands why. He was deeply influenced by the Bible, and the following lines are typical of him:

> In memory of the fallen, in memory of all
> who, even if not forgotten, have no headstones,
> lying unreproachfully, their mouths agape,
> without an epitaph, without a cross.
> ....
> There is no place of exile for me
> either in heaven or in hell.
> The investigation is long,
> it is a simple matter to find out
> who is guilty:
> a mountain of bones.
> Oh Lord, it is not worth judging men....
> Wipe happiness or wrath from your face....
> for life and death are eternal......[30]

Till the very end Brodsky remained faithful to his religious inspiration, and when asked by his judges in court: "Did you learn to become a poet?" he replied: "I never thought that such a thing could be achieved by education...I have always believed that it came from God."[31] When one reads Anna Akhmatova's "Requiem," which deals with the torments endured by Mother Earth, one realizes that it is the most poetic and at the same time the most religious Russian literary work of the 20th century.

The examples given above provide some indication of the new trends towards spiritual content in Soviet literature, and bring home with considerable clarity the contrast between the evolution of this literature during the '50's and '60's and the period prior to the death of Stalin. Vladimir Soloukhin expresses this "reaching for the stars" and for new horizons of feeling with the words: "To live on earth and yet to strive for heaven. Such is man's sweet lot."[32]

---

[29] *Grani*, No. 51, 1962, p. 5.
[30] Iosif Brodsky, *Stikhotvoreniya i poemy* (Verse and Poems), Washington-New York, 1965, p. 180.
[31] *Ibid.*, p. 5.
[32] V. Soloukhin, *op. cit.*, p. 23.

Summary

Max Hayward

I would like to enlarge the framework of the questions that have come under discussion. A larger view of things seems necessary if only because we have sometimes tended to talk about Russia as if it were like the city of Lyubimov in Abram Tertz's story—that is, as if it were separated from the rest of the world by a kind of mental barrier and were not part of a common European or world culture, and existed in spiritual and intellectual isolation. Of course, this was true for a certain time—that is, under Stalin. From the middle 'thirties until Stalin's death Russia was indeed isolated from the outside world. We are all aware of the methods Stalin employed to achieve this end. He achieved it very simply by terrorising the population and making people afraid to speak to one another, to speak with foreigners, or to have any contact whatsoever with the outside world. This is all true. But since his death thirteen years have gone by and Russia no longer lives in isolation. In our discussions we were right to assume that the situation in Russia is *sui generis* and that there are specific conditions in Russia that do not exist in other countries. But these conditions are changing very rapidly. The most important thing is that during the past decade Russia has again begun to commune with the outside world in many ways and has begun the business of absorbing modern concepts, modern ideas. All this is happening quietly, often "underground," but it is happening nevertheless. A person living in Moscow or Leningrad, or even in Kiev or Kharkov, now has much easier access to Western literature, and hence to Western ideas, not to mention Western broadcasts, to which he is freer to listen than ever before. So it is perhaps wrong to think of "Soviet man" as a being who differs so much from us that he should be examined as if he were an exotic animal. Furthermore, the quest for new values, particularly in the field of philosophy, is not unique to Russia. A similar kind of search is under way in other countries. I have just read a very interesting article in the *New York Times Magazine* by the American philosopher and sociologist, Louis Feuer, entitled "American Philosophy is Dead." In essence he speaks here about American philosophy more or less in the same vein in which we have spoken about ideology in the Soviet Union. He says that the 2,000 American philosophers teaching in American universities could disappear one fine day and no one would miss them, since what they are teaching is of no significance. This, he says, is because they are concerned with linguistic analysis, and have retreated into a barren scholasticism reminiscent of the middle ages. But it is even worse than medieval scholasticism because the problems concerned are even more trivial and are quite irrelevant to the ontological questions that exercise the young, questions that philosophy should be attempting to answer. For this reason (as in Russia) young people look to literature

130

rather than to philosophy for an answer to their questions. Feuer also notes the interesting fact that in recent years more and more people are turning to, or at least, showing respect for the theologians. They feel that the questions put forward by theologians in America come much closer to the fundamental problems of being than the futile hairsplitting of the philosophers. In America, Europe, and Russia the searchings that are currently going on are not identical, but they are similar. The fact that Russians are also concerned with a renewed search for the answer to fundamental problems seems to me to be in itself symptomatic of their cultural re-integration with the outside world.

What are the distinguishing features of the situation in Russia? Because of her isolation under Stalin, Russia has lagged behind in many respects, and she now has to make up for lost time—something like thirty years were lost. During this time, certain trends of thought which became commonplace in Western Europe were suppressed in Russia and still have to be absorbed into Russian culture. This is true, for instance, of Freudism, which is still officially taboo, although Freud is well known to Soviet specialists in psychiatry and his works were available in Russian translation in the 'twenties. His assimilation into the broader cultural background of educated Russians proceeds only slowly and underground. On the other hand, as far as modern literature is concerned, there has been quite remarkable progress in recent years. Some of Kafka has been translated, and there is talk of republishing some of James Joyce's works (he was published in Russian in the 'twenties and 'thirties). Ionesco's *Rhinoceros* has recently appeared in translation and is being rehearsed by the *Sovremennik* Theatre.

But what matters is that new ideas and artistic concepts are finding their way into Russia and have begun, if not to dominate, at least to influence the minds of the younger generation. At the same time—and even more important— they are re-examining their own past, their own traditions, including the traditions of the 1920's, when Russian literature flourished under the Bolsheviks.

The most significant development in Russia after the death of Stalin has been, of course, the disintegration of Marxism-Leninism.

I would like to clarify something I said during the discussion on the first day, and I owe an apology to Karl Marx and Father Wetter. I have compared Marxism-Leninism, on which Father Wetter has written a book, with a dead dinosaur. This might suggest that the book is about something that is no longer of any interest, about an antediluvian animal. This was a bad way of putting it. I should stress that Father Wetter's book is concerned not with paleozoology, but with the natural history, as it were, of an artificially preserved dinosaur which made its home in a country of corresponding dimensions in 1917. And if this dinosaur had not settled in Russia and taken on a new lease of life, I am sure that it would have died a natural death at the end of the last century or at the beginning of this century, because it was already on its last legs and it would have been killed off in Russia—people like Berdyaev were putting an end to it. But, thanks to the Revolution, the dinosaur survived until our time, or in any event it managed to linger on until the death of Stalin. As far as Marxism is concerned—as distinct

131

from Marxism-Leninism—I must say that just as, whether one believes in the theory of evolution or not, a little bit of the dinosaur is still in all of us, so the same may be said of Marx—namely, that something of him remains in all of us, insofar as he had an influence on the minds of the last century. As we know, Marx stood Hegel on his head and shook the dialectics out of his pocket. Then he took a little from English economists and even something from French utopians, and from this he manufactured his Marxism. Then Lenin added a pinch of Russian populism and a large dose of Nechaev to this peculiar concoction and Bolshevism was the result. Thanks to Lenin's legerdemain and the disintegration of the Russian social system in 1917, thanks to the war which was then raging in Europe, this dinosaur settled in Russia and has been there ever since. But in the end it was artificially kept in being, and by the time of Stalin's death, it also was really dead. Stalin stifled it.

The dinosaur, just as any other animal, needs air, and Marxism died of suffocation in Russia. It died not only because of the Russian disorderliness mentioned by Bishop Nafaniel, but also as a result of the cruel measures Stalin used against people who tried to develop and adapt Marxism. Moreover, Marxism, like any other doctrine, cannot survive in isolation, without competition. It is extremely important for any teaching that it be free to compete with rivals. I once had an interesting conversation with a Soviet scholar on the subject of Marxism in Russia. I said that we in the West were naturally anxious to have an intellectual "dialogue" with Russia, but that one major obstacle was that the Russians were *not even Marxists*, that there was not even the common language of Marxism between Russia and the West. I made the point that what was useful in Marxism (for instance, its emphasis on economic and social factors in the study of history) had been absorbed into the Western European consciousness, and that Western intellectuals were conversant with the language of Marxism, just as they are with the language of Freudism. Unfortunately, however, what started out in the West as a hypothesis had in Russia degenerated into dogma, and thus destroyed itself. The Soviet scholar appeared to agree with me and said: "Yes, you are right, of course. We have no Marxism. We have Marxism-Leninism. There is a big difference."

As a result of Stalin's destruction of Marxism, a terrible vacuum was formed. A vacuum also exists in the West, as Feuer points out. Here, too, therefore, people are engaged in a frantic search for answers to fundamental questions. But it seems to me that the situation in Russia is far worse because of the suddenness with which belief in official dogma was shattered. There is plenty of testimony in literature to the psychological shock that occurred among Soviet young people: you only need to read Yevtushenko's "Precocious Autobiography," in which he describes how he suddenly lost his faith on the day of Stalin's funeral. For the young this collapse of a world picture in which many of them had believed was not accompanied by the freedom to turn to the outside world in order to fill in the abyss which now opened before them. They were not given the freedom to discuss openly, with a view to seeking new ideas of potential interest to them, the intellectual developments which had been going on abroad during all the decades of Russia's cultural isolation. By "ideas," I mean simply philosophical ones, not political ones. Not having an opportunity to discuss freely anything new and being in a situation in which one has to continue to pay lip service to a dead ideology—this is what is frightening. It is also frustrating to be subjected to enforced, though now only partial, cultural isolation at a time when access to the outside world has improved because of radio broadcasts, tourist and student exchanges, etc. The whole business of "catching up" culturally still has to be conducted almost "underground," in conditions in which you can get into trouble for disseminating manuscripts. If your manuscript reaches the West and gets printed, as we have seen in the recent case of Daniel and Sinyavsky, you can wind up in prison camp. Feuer says that in America there are 2,000 useless philosophers (though I am sure that not all of them spend their time pursuing trivia), but in Russia there are myriads of agitators and propagandists, a whole army of lecturers and university professors who teach a dead dogma in which nobody believes. There can be no question here of faith; Marxism-Leninism has ceased (at least in Russia) to have an even quasi-religious attraction. People have to seek an answer to their vital questions within themselves, generally by them-selves, and sometimes in groups or circles. The main thing is that people are increasingly able to establish contact with one another, to exchange ideas, etc. The intellectual community is no longer atomized, as it was some years ago.

The impressive amount of factual material reported to us at this symposium shows us that all this is true. If published sources are combined with eyewitness accounts by foreigners who have lived in Russia, then we can obtain a very clear picture of the situation. The basic facts are not a matter of argument, though when it comes to the evaluation of these facts, argument is both possible and inevitable. What, for example, is most likely to fill the vacuum left by the death of the ideology? Well, we have an approximate idea of the range of ideas to which Russians are, albeit "underground," exposed. We know of their interest in existentialism and Berdyaev. Incidentally, two or three years ago *Voprosy filosofii* (Questions of Philosophy) suddenly started a polemic against Berdyaev. This was because Berdyaev had been quoted in the *Zhurnal Moskovskoy Patriarkhii* (Journal of the Moscow Patriarchate). The editors of *Voprosy filosofii* were evidently horrified because they had always counted on a low level of philoso-phical thinking in the Russian Orthodox Church. This low level is, of course,—like the degradation of the Church at a more material level—deliberately engi-neered. This panic over the use of more sophisticated arguments in the usually very tame *Journal of the Moscow Patriarchate* is symptomatic and revealing. The fact that *Voprosy filosofii* felt it necessary to answer back would only, of course, heighten interest in Berdyaev. Then, naturally, there is interest in logical positivism which, according to Feuer, has become sterile in the West. But, whatever direction it may take, the search for new ideas and values is done gropingly and even, to a certain extent, blindfold. Religion occupies a large part of this search, and, of course, every such quest takes on religious forms. In this connection, the question of whether young people go to church or not and in what numbers seems to me

133

to be relatively unimportant. It has been said that, as everywhere else, it is mostly old people who go to church and that young people do not go to church either in Russia or the West,—well, perhaps they will when they grow old. But the point is that we have certain proof that the spiritual gropings of the young do sometimes take on religious or semi-religious forms. All this is reflected in Soviet literature, as Mme. Shakhovskaya has so well demonstrated. Indeed, the whole process of intellectual and cultural renewal is best seen in creative literature.

As far as the ultimate potential of this process is concerned, there are, of course, two sides, as always in such discussions: people are divided into pessimists and optimists. In my opinion this is not a fruitful division, because we cannot know what will happen in the future. Whether the ascertainable facts are seen in an optimistic or pessimistic light depends on the temperament of the individual observer. I myself am inclined to be "optimistic," notwithstanding the limitations placed on the intellectual ferment by its apparent confinement to the capitals, Moscow and Leningrad, and to a section of the intelligentsia. According to the official Soviet definition, the "intelligentsia" represents all those who in the West would be classified as professional people, (engineers, doctors, etc.) and of course only a part of this intelligentsia is concerned with the old "accursed questions." But I am confident that there are many Soviet intellectuals—far more than is evident on the surface—who are caught up in the ferment but are reluctant, for obvious reasons, to give any overt sign of interest in any other than their strictly professional problems.

We have seen in Poland and now even in Czechoslovakia (I say "even," because Czechoslovakia in its post-Stalin development has until now been the most backward of the satellite countries in many respects), an almost complete inner emancipation of the intelligentsia from the trammels of dead dogma. When you speak with Poles, of course, you do not feel that there are any barriers to normal intellectual discourse. If in Russia the pace of change is proceeding more slowly than in Poland and Czechoslovakia this is largely because the Russians have been isolated much longer and because normal political and intellectual reflexes have been much more systematically distorted.

Another concomitant factor which distinguishes the situation in Russia in the present uncertain period of transition is that because of their long isolation people are more easily confused by the sheer divergency and variety of the new ideas and intellectual and cultural stimuli which are beginning to crowd in on them. When a country is in a state of what might be called cultural shock it is difficult to pick and choose from among the various alternative view-points which come in from abroad or well up from some long supressed internal source. The effect of this bewilderment can be to produce a certain skepticism or even cynicism. In other people a healthy skepticism is likely to yield to an overwhelming desire to find some all-embracing system or creed to replace the one that has crumbled to dust. The great temptation of the Russian intelligentsia has always been to seek total, man-made solutions to empirical problems. The whole of the 19th century is littered with the debris of borrowed and ready-made systems. It may be hoped that after the disastrous flirtation with Marxism, which turned into a deadly embrace, Russian intellectuals may be more wary of the kind of intellectual maximalism against which Pasternak warns so eloquently in *Dr. Zhivago*.

The great value of this symposium has been to throw light on the beginnings of a process, the end of which we cannot know, and which it would be arrogant to try to foretell. What is certain, however, is that Russia is seeking fresh bearings which will take her in a new, and probably more hopeful, direction than in the past.